THE MEDIEVAL LIBRARY UNDER
THE GENERAL EDITORSHIP OF
SIR ISRAEL GOLLANCZ, Litt.D., F.B.A.

THE CHRONICLE OF JOCELIN
OF BRAKELOND

Seal of Abbot Samson.
(*Slightly enlarged. The length of the*)
original is 3½ inches.

THE CHRONICLE OF JOCELIN OF BRAKE-LOND, MONK OF ST. EDMUNDSBURY:

A PICTURE OF MONASTIC AND SOCIAL LIFE IN THE XIITH CENTURY NEWLY TRANSLATED AND EDITED BY L. C. JANE, INTRODUCTION BY CARDINAL GASQUET

COOPER SQUARE PUBLISHERS, INC.
NEW YORK
1966

"A VERITABLE MONK OF BURY ST. EDMUNDS IS
WORTH ATTENDING TO, IF BY CHANCE MADE VISIBLE
AND AUDIBLE. HERE HE IS; AND IN HIS HAND A
MAGICAL SPECULUM, MUCH GONE TO RUST, INDEED,
YET IN FRAGMENTS STILL CLEAR; WHEREIN THE
MARVELLOUS IMAGE OF HIS EXISTENCE DOES STILL
SHADOW ITSELF, THOUGH FITFULLY, AND AS WITH
AN INTERMITTENT LIGHT."

Carlyle: Past and Present. Book II., Chapter 1.

Published 1966 by Cooper Square Publishers, Inc.
59 Fourth Avenue, New York, N. Y. 10003
Library of Congress Catalog Card No. 66-23318

Printed in the United States of America
by Noble Offset Printers Inc., New York, N. Y. 10003

INTRODUCTION

Few mediæval documents have excercised a greater
fascination over men's minds in these latter days than
" The Chronicle of Jocelin of Brakelond." More
than sixty years ago the publication of the Latin text
of this history, by the Camden Society, attracted the
attention of the great Thomas Carlyle, and furnished
him with material for sketching his picture of " The
Ancient Monk," which occupied the entire second
book of his *Past and Present*. Although the modern
sage in his own rugged way affected no little contempt
for what he called this " extremely foreign book," and
for the " monk-Latin " in which it was written, it is
evident that Jocelin's simple story of the wise, firm,
yet withal gentle rule of a mediæval abbot over a great
English monastery cast a spell over him, the influence
of which can be detected in every page of his delight-
ful and almost surprisingly sympathetic account of
Abbot Samson and of Edmundsbury.

In this case the *Past*, as Carlyle read it in the "Chronicle," was so entirely different from the *Present*, as he knew it in his day, that the wonder is not that he was fascinated by it, but that he was able with its help to paint so true and living a picture and to fashion so fitting a frame in which to set it. For to him, without doubt, the story dealt with what he regarded as "vanished existences"—"ideas, life-furniture, whole workings and ways," which were not only *Past*, but gone beyond recall, and "covered deeper than Pompeii with the lava-ashes and inarticulate wreck of seven hundred years!"

And indeed it cannot be denied that the ideals and aspirations as revealed to us in the history of Abbot Samson and, so far as we know, in the life story of his biographer Jocelin, are of a higher and almost a different order to those of our modern world. To men of their calling in those far-off times, the natural and the supernatural were united and intermingled in the simplest and most ordinary way. Their very notions of the unseen world are almost sufficient to take away the breath of those whose lots have been cast in this more material and prosaic age of doubts and disbeliefs. To Samson, and Jocelin, and their fellow-monks at Edmundsbury in the twelfth century, heaven, as a great writer has said of earlier English monasticism, was hardly even "next door." The future life was merely the present continued, and each man went forth to his task as it came and laboured at it day by day, not with any idea of finishing it, but only of carrying it on for the span of his allotted existence. They built, and planted, and wrote till the end came, and then they went to heaven and others stepped into their places and took up the common work. It was indeed a "simple life": it was almost Arcadian in its picturesque simplicity, and, as Cardinal Newman says of the same life in the days of our Venerable Bede, it reminds us of those times in the dayspring of the world, when Adam delved and Abel watched the flocks, and Noah tended his vines, and angels visited them.

This living belief in the nearness and all-importance of the supernatural is the key-note of Jocelin's charming story of a few brief years in the long history of an old English abbey, a new translation of which is here given to the public. As a story, however, Brakelond's "Chronicle" is not wholly, nor indeed mostly, either mysterious or incredible: there are troubles, and trials, and difficulties enough recounted by the writer; and at every turn we may see evidences of human nature and even of human struggles and passions, which are sufficient, and as some may perhaps think, more than sufficient, to show us that it is a history of men, and not of angels, which the old monk is setting forth so naturally and so truthfully. At any rate, there is quite sufficient of the human element in the narrative to give most of us a human interest in the story.

And this itself is proof that Jocelin is a true chronicler of what really took place, and no mere romancer tempted to edit or suppress entirely what might not be unto "edification." He manifests no desire to make himself or his brethren appear other than what they were in reality—that is, thorough Englishmen, with strong wills and human passions, which though these same passions might occasionally appear to gain the mastery, they were at all times endeavouring to subdue unto God's service by the help of His grace and through the broad-minded provisions of St. Benedict's Rule. The actors who appear in this living drama, though they are for the most part monks, are obviously men, natural and human enough in all their works and words; but these men are at the same time also monks, endeavouring to raise their minds and hearts to supernatural ideals. and striving to attain to that personal communion with God which is the aim and object of all true religion and of all religious observance and practice. This is "another world truly," writes Carlyle, "and this present poor distressed world might get some profit by looking wisely into it, instead of foolishly. But at lowest, O dilettante friend, let us know always that it *was* a world, and not a void infinite of grey haze with phantasms swimming in it. These old St. Edmundsbury walls, I say, were not peopled with phantasms, but with men of flesh and blood, made altogether as we are. Had thou and I then been who knows but we ourselves had taken refuge from an evil Time and fled to dwell here, and meditate on an Eternity, in such fashion as we could? Alas, how like an old osseous fragment, a broken blackened shin-bone of the old dead Ages, this black ruin looks out, not yet covered by the soil; still indicating what a once gigantic Life lies buried there! It is dead now, and dumb; but was alive once and spake. For twenty generations, here was the earthly arena where painful living men worked out their life-wrestle,— looked at by Earth, by Heaven and Hell. Bells tolled to prayers; and men of many humours, various thoughts, chanted Vespers and Matins;—and round the little islet of their life rolled for ever (as round ours still rolls, though we were blind and deaf) the illimitable Ocean, tinting all things with *its* eternal hues and reflexes, making strange prophetic music! How silent now!"

The Author.—Jocelin de Brakelond, the writer of the Chronicle called by his name, was a monk of Edmundsbury. The date of his birth is uncertain, but as he became a novice in that abbey in 1173, we may suppose that he was born not later than 1156. It has been conjectured that he was a native of Bury St. Edmunds, and that his name Brakelond was derived from that of an ancient street of the city, in accordance with the common practise of calling monks by the name of the place from which they came to religion. Little more is known about him than he tells us incidentally in the course of his narrative, but one of his contemporaries in the monastery speaks of him as "a man of excellent religious observance, as well as a power both in word and work"—*eximiae religionis, potens sermone et opere.* Carlyle sees him in his writing as a man of a "patient, peaceable, loving, clear-smiling nature." A "wise simplicity," he adds, "is in him; much natural sense; a veracity that goes deeper than words." What more can we desire in a writer, especially when we may add that he shows himself to have been a cultured man, acquainted with the ancient authors, quoting Virgil and Horace and Ovid? His knowledge of the Bible is naturally extensive, and, as was common in those days, his very phraseology is obviously founded upon the sacred text. He once likewise cites, with acknowledgment, a short passage from the more modern Ralph de Diceto's *Imagines Historiarum*. Our latter-dry philosopher praises him also because he shows himself to have "a pleasant wit; and to love a timely joke, though in a mild subdued manner; very amiable to see."

In A.D. 1173, as just noted, Jocelin entered the community, and passed under the care of Samson of Tottington, who subsequently became abbot, but who was then Master of novices. The then abbot, Hugh, was old, and although a high standard of the religious exercises and of the monastic life inside the cloister was maintained, the temporalities were in a sad state, and year by year tended to get from bad to worse, so that Jocelin's early experiences of monastic life were connected with anxieties about the load of debt to money-lenders under which Edmundsbury groaned.

He tells us that he had himself seen bonds for re-
payment made out to the Jews, under which, for
failure to meet the sums falling due, the original loan
had grown in eight years from £100 to £800. No
wonder that the youthful religious questioned his
Master of novices as to why some remedy was not
found by those in authority for a state of things
which meant temporal ruin and disgrace for the
community of Edmundsbury.

In 1180 Abbot Hugh met with an accident and
died. After a period of a year and three months the
former Master of novices, Samson, then the provident
Sacrist, was chosen in his place. It was during this
period of vacancy that, in recording something which
happened in the monastery, Jocelin incidentally makes
mention of another literary work of his own, namely,
the *Book of the Miracles of St. Robert*, a boy supposed to
have been martyred by the Jews in 1181, who was
entombed in the church at Edmundsbury.

On the election of Samson, Jocelin was appointed
his chaplain, and this brought him into the closest
connection with the abbot for six years. In 1198 and
1200 he was Guest-master, and in 1212 he held the
office of Almoner. In all these offices the future
chronicler had exceptional means of acquiring in-

formation, and these he utilised in writing the story of Abbot Samson's administration, which is introduced by a vivid sketch of the temporal disorder of the house in the closing years of Abbot Hugh.   His Chronicle covers the period of the history of Edmundsbury from 1173 to 1190, and, as he says in the beginining, "he took care to write only what he himself saw and heard."   The date of his death is uncertain.

The "Chronicle."—The Latin text of *Cronica Joceline* is found complete only in one manuscript— Harl. MS. 1005—in the British Museum.   It was printed for the first time by the Camden Society in 1840 under the editorship of I. G. Gage Rokewood, who supplied a valuable Introduction and notes, of which subsequent editors have availed themselves. The text was likewise printed in Mr. Thomas Arnold's *Memorials of St. Edmund's Abbey* (Rolls Series) I., pp. 209-336.

In 1844, under the title *Monastic and Social Life in the Twelfth Century, as exemplified in the Chronicle of Jocelin of Brakelond, A.D.* 1173 - 1202, the work was translated by Thomas Edlyne Tomlins.   Carlyle's work, *Past and Present*, published in 1843 had already drawn attention to the "Chronicle of Jocelin," and another edition of Mr. Tomlin's work was called for in 1849. This translation has since appeared at least once, but for the present edition a new English version has been carefully prepared from the original Latin text of the Chronicle.

Abbot Samson.—The central figure and, as we may say, "the hero" of Jocelin's story is, of course, Abbot Samson. He was born in 1135 at Tottington, near Thetford, in Norfolk. His father appears to have died when Samson was young, and a pretty legend of a boyish dream in which St. Edmund extended his protection to the child against the assults of the devil, and the recognition of the place seen in the dream as the gate of the monastery of St. Edmundsbury, when his mother had taken him with her on a pilgrimage to the shrine of the saint, led to his taking refuge in the cloister. He had received his early instruction from a schoolmaster named William of Diss, and he attained the degree of Master of Arts in the University of Paris. In this place we are not concerned with the events of his life: these may be read for the most part in the Chronicle of Jocelin of Brakelond. What alone seems to be called for in this brief Introduction is some account of his person and character as it is manifested in the scattered evidences of his acts.

If we want a picture of the man let us take Carlyle's, who sketches "the substantial figure of a man
with eminent nose, bushy brows, and clear-flashing
eyes, his russet beard growing daily greyer," and his
hair which before his elevation to the abbot's chair,
had been black, becoming daily more and more silvered
with his many cares. We know something of the task
that was before him when he gathered up the reins of
office and we may be sure he knew more. But as we
see him in the pages of Jocelin, he was not the man
to flinch from his duty, or to seek to let difficulties
mend themselves by pretending that he did not see
them. From the time that he walked barefooted into
his church to be installed in the abbatial chair, he let
all see that he was abbot and had come to rule. He
had set his whole strength to accomplish a great task
and his shoulders to sustain an almost overwhelming
burden, when in the hour of his election he walked to
the altar singing the *Miserere mei* with his brethren.
"His head was held erect," says the faithful Jocelin,
"and his face showed no change," a portent which
called from the king the remark: "This abbot-elect
seems to think himself capable of governing an abbey."

"It is beautiful"—writes Carlyle in a philosophical
appreciation of the principles of monastic government

—"it is beautiful how the chrysalis governing-soul, shaking off its dusty slough and prison, starts forth winged, a true royal soul! Our new abbot has a right honest, unconscious feeling, without insolence as without fear or flutter, of what he is and what others are. A courage to quell the proudest, an honest pity to encourage the humblest. Withal there is a noble reticence in this Lord Abbot : much vain unreason he hears ; lays up without response. He is not there to expect reason and nobleness of others, he is there to give them of his own reason and nobleness. Is he not their servant, who can suffer from them and for them ; bear the burden their poor spindle-limbs totter and stagger under ; and in virtue of *being* their servant, govern them, lead them out of weakness to strength, out of defeat into victory ?"

Abbot Samson ruled over his house for thirty years, and when in 1212, ten years after the end of Jocelin's Chronicle, he died, he was followed to the grave by a sorrowing community whose unstinted reverence and affection he had won. An unknown monk of Edmundsbury, the author of another Chronicle of the house, thus wrote of him : "On the 30th December, at St. Edmund's, died Samson, of pious memory, the venerable abbot of that place ; after he had prosperously ruled the abbey committed to him for thirty years and had freed it from a load of debt, had enriched it with privileges, liberties, possessions and spacious buildings and had restored the worship of the church both internally and externally, in the most ample manner. Then bidding his last farewell to his sons, by whom the blessed man deserved to be blest for evermore, whilst they were all standing by and gazing with awe at a death which was a cause for admiration, not for regret, in the fourth year of the interdict he rested in peace."

The first business to which Abbot Samson applied himself after his election was the task of understanding and grappling with the deplorable financial state of his house. He insisted upon the immediate production of every claim against the monastery, and by personally visiting each of its many manors he gained a correct knowledge of its resources. Within twelve months he had formed his plans and had quieted every creditor: within twelve years the entire debt had been paid off, and he could turn his attention to building and adorning the house of St Edmund. It is impossible to read the pages of Jocelin without seeing that the ruling idea of the abbot's life was his devotion to his great patron, St. Edmund. He was the servant, after God, of the saint, his representative and the upholder of his honour and privileges, the champion of his rights, the guardian of his property. Inspired by this thought he worked to make Edmundsbury worthy of its patron, and in his success he saw the result of the saint's intercession and protection.

"Apart from this special devotion to St. Edmund, it is easy to see," writes Mr. Thomas Arnold, "that Samson was an earnestly religious man, and not a Christian by halves. After the news had come of the capture of Jerusalem by the Saracens, Samson took the loss of the Holy Places so much to heart, that from that time he wore undergarments of hair-cloth and abstained from the use of meat."

He was, too, a thorough Englishman, and read admirably — *elegantissime* — the Bible in English — *scripturam anglice scriptam* — and "he was wont to preach to the people in English—but in the dialect of Norfolk where he had been born and bred." On one occasion he gives as a reason, and as some may think, a somewhat strange reason, for appointing a monk to an office, that "he did not know French." He was no doubt anxious to secure that St. Edmundsbury should be truly national, with its roots deep in the soil of his country, to teach it to build up its own traditions, and to let people see that it was a great *English* house.

But Samson's work was not accomplished without grave anxiety, none the less because it was unseen by others. Though he walked upright with a smiling face, and had ever the courage to battle for the rights of his house when there was need, in a way that might make people regard him as a man of iron nerve possessed of a soul that never felt any trouble, nevertheless in the first fourteen years of his administration his black hair was blanched as white as snow, and Jocelin speaks of hearing his beloved master walking about when all were in bed and relieving his pent-up feelings with sighs and groans. Once the chronicler took courage to tell his master that he had thus heard him in his night vigil, and to this the abbot replied : "'Tis no wonder : you (as my chaplain) share in the sweets of my office, in the meat and drink, in the journeys and the like, but you little think what I have to do to provide for my house and family, or of the many and difficult matters of my pastoral office, which are always pressing upon me : these are the things which make my soul anxious and cause me to sigh."

And so when Abbot Samson came to die, the thin veil which to him and his monks of Edmundsbury alone hid the world to come from their vision was parted, and the supernatural life eternal was revealed to him in the most natural of ways. He passed from labour for God and St. Edmundsbury, to rest in God and with his loved patron, carrying with him the full sheaves of his good works. Carlyle has only partially caught the idea when he writes: "Genuine work alone, what thou workest faithfully, that is eternal." "Yes," he concludes, "a noble Abbot Samson resigns himself to oblivion; feels it no hardship, but a comfort; counts it as a still resting-place, for much sick fret, and fever, and stupidity, which in the night-watches often made his strong heart sigh."

FRANCIS AIDAN GASQUET,
Abbot-President of the English Benedictines.

THE AUTHOR'S PREFACE

I HAVE undertaken to write of those things which I have seen and heard, and which have occured in the church of Saint Edmund, from the year in which the Flemings were taken without the town, in which year also I assumed the religious habit, and in which Prior Hugh was deposed and Robert made Prior in his room. And I have related the evil as a warning, and the good for an example.

TABLE OF CONTENTS

	PAGE
INTRODUCTION	ix
THE AUTHOR'S PREFACE	xxv

THE CHRONICLE OF JOCELIN OF BRAKELOND :—

How abbot Hugh ruled the church of St. Edmund	1
How the monastery was freed from legatine visitation	6
Concerning master Dennis the cellarer .	7
How abbot Hugh strove to win the favour of master Samson	9
How abbot Hugh came by his death . .	10
How the death of abbot Hugh was told to the king, and of those things which the servants of the king did	11
How the prior ruled the monastery, while there was no abbot	12
How the cellarer and the sacristan behaved during the vacancy	13
Concerning the conduct of Samson the sub-sacristan during the vacancy . . .	13

PAGE

How the enemies of Samson prevailed against
him, but only for a time   .   .   .   15

How the monks disputed among themselves
which of them should be abbot   .   .   16

How Samson the subsacristan bore himself
while others discussed the vacancy   .   .   21

How the author spoke his mind too
hastily   21

How the archbishop of Norway dwelt in the
abbot's lodgings while the abbacy was
vacant   23

Of the martyrdom of Saint Robert   .   .   23

How thirteen men were chosen, by command
of the king, to elect an abbot in the presence
of the king   24

How Samson suggested that the monastery
should appoint men to make a secret choice
of an abbot, and how this was done   .   .   25

How, on the advice of Samson, it was decided
what should be done if the king would not
grant freedom of election   .   .   .   27

How the chosen thirteen journeyed to the
king   28

Of the dreams which the brothers dreamed
concerning the election of a new abbot   .   29

CONTENTS

PAGE

How the thirteen came to the king and
showed to him the names of those whom
the confessors had selected . . . 31

How the thirteen, by command of the king,
chose three other names from the monastery and three strangers 33

How the list of names was reduced from nine
to two 34

How Samson was elected abbot . . . 34

How the news of the election came to the
monastery, and how Samson was blessed . 36

How Samson, having been made abbot,
returned and was received at the monastery 37

How abbot Samson began to rule the monastery 40

How the abbot met the demand of Thomas
de Hastings that his nephew should be
steward 42

How the abbot dealt with the lands of his
house 43

Of that which was done at the abbot's first
chapter 46

How certain men wished to conspire against
the abbot 47

PAGE

How the abbot journeyed through the lands of Saint Edmund, and how he escaped death at Warkton 48

How the creditors of the abbey demanded payment, and how the abbot took his manors into his own hand . . . 49

How the abbot did not then take Harlow into his own hand 50

How the abbot managed the lands which he farmed himself 51

How abbot Samson was made a justice, and how he bore himself in this office . . 52

How some men made complaint against the abbot 54

How the author talked with the abbot concerning the sadness of his manner . . 56

Concerning a dream which the abbot had when a boy 58

How the abbot restrained his temper that he might not offend 59

How the abbot forbade secret accusations, and how he ordered the restoration of all private seals 60

Concerning further regulations which the abbot made 61

PAGE

Concerning the appearance and private character of the abbot 62

How abbot Samson dealt with flatterers . 65

How abbot Samson managed his household . 66

How the abbot treated those monks with
whom he had been intimate before he
became abbot 67

How the abbot treated his relations . . 69

How the abbot was mindful of those who
had shown kindness to him in the past,
and how he treated those who had been
harsh 70

Concerning other good acts of abbot Samson 72

How the Jews were driven from Saint
Edmund's 73

How the abbot secured the manor of Mildenhall, and endowed the hospital at
Babwell 74

Concerning the church of Woolpit, and how
it was secured for the abbey . . . 76

How the abbot disputed with the archbishop
concerning the manor of Eleigh . . 80

How the abbot wished to take the cross, and
how he offered to seek king Richard in
Germany 85

PAGE

How the abbot resisted the authority of the
legate 86

Of the conduct of the abbot while king
Richard was in captivity . . . 86

Concerning that which befel certain knights
who desired to hold a tournament contrary
to the wish of the abbot 87

Concerning the missions of the abbot to the
papal court 89

How the abbot met the claim of Earl de
Clare to bear the standard of Saint Edmund 90

Concerning the case of Adam de Cokefield . 92

How the mill which Herbert the dean had
built was overturned 94

How the right of the abbot to present to
certain churches was disputed, and what
befel in the matter 95

How abbot Samson disputed with Jordan de
Ros 97

How the author made a list of the abbot's
churches as a gift to the abbot, and the
names of those churches 99

How the abbot freed his church from contri-
bution to the fine inflicted on Norfolk and
Suffolk 103

CONTENTS

PAGE

How the abbot disputed with his knights . 104

Concerning Henry of Essex . . . 108

How the abbot deceived the bishop of Ely
for the good of his church . . . 113

How there were disputes concerning the
appointment of bailiffs for the town . 114

How abbot Samson disputed with the men
of London about the payment of tolls . 119

How there was a dispute with the burghers
as to the dues from the town . . . 121

Concerning the charter granted to the town
by the abbot 123

How the monastery was troubled with incompetent cellarers 125

How the abbot resisted Hubert Walker when
he claimed legatine authority over the abbey 128

How the abbot contended with his knights
as to service across the sea . . . 134

How the abbot took charge of the cellar, and
how for that cause murmuring arose in the
monastery 137

Concerning the will of Hamo Blund . . 144

How there were riots in the cemetery, and
concerning that which was done in the
matter 145

CONTENTS

PAGE

How the monks were restored to Coventry . 147

How the abbot endowed schools at Saint
Edmund's 149

Concerning improvements which the abbot
made in the abbey 150

How the abbot disputed with the king as to
the wardship of the land of Adam de
Cokefield 153

How the customary dues of the town were
changed 155

Concerning a dispute between the cellarer
and the sacristan 157

Concerning the customs and dues of the cellarer 160

How the author was blamed for praising the
abbot too much 164

How there was a fire near the shrine of Saint
Edmund 166

How the abbot attributed the fire to the
greed of the monks 171

Concerning the dream that a certain great
person had, and how the abbot interpreted
the same 172

How the monks interpreted the dream in a
different way, and how they angered the
abbot on that account 173

CONTENTS

PAGE

Concerning the translation of the body of
Saint Edmund 174

How king John visited the abbey soon after
his accession 181

Concerning the dispute between the porter
and the monks 182

How disturbances arose in the monastery, and of the end to which they
came 184

Concerning the knights of Saint Edmund
and their fiefs 187

Concerning the manors of Geoffrey Ruffus,
and the cellar 190

Concerning that which occured on the death
of Adam de Cokefield 192

How the abbot received the abbot of Cluny 194

How Robert the prior died, and of the dis-
cussions as to his successor . . . 194

How Heribert was elected prior . . 197

How the author reflected on the choice of
Heribert 201

How the unlearned brothers mocked those
that were learned 202

How the abbot was not perfect . . . 203

Concerning the fishponds of Babwell . . 204

PAGE

Whether it is better to have an abbot from
  one's own house 205

How there was a quarrel with the monks of
  Ely 206

How the abbot disputed with the bishop of
  Ely 210

How king John summoned the abbot to him,
  and of that which was done thereupon . 211

How the abbot left the monastery in peace
  with all men 213

NOTES. 217

TABLE OF DATES 243

LIST OF THE ABBOTS OF ST. EDMUND'S . 247

INDEX. 249

THE CHRONICLE OF JOCELIN
OF BRAKELOND

HOW ABBOT HUGH RULED THE CHURCH
OF ST. EDMUND

IN those days Abbot Hugh grew old, and his eyes, were dim. He was a good and kindly man, a godfearing and pious monk, but in temporal matters he was unskilful and improvident. He relied too much on his own intimates and believed too readily in them, rather trusting to a stranger's advice than using his own judgment. It is true that discipline and the service of God, and all that pertained to the rule, flourised greatly within the cloister, but without the walls all things were mismanaged. For every man, seeing that he served a simple and ageing lord, did not that which was right, but that which was pleasing in his own eyes. The townships and all the hundreds of the abbot were given to farm; the woods were destroyed, and the houses on the manors were on the

A.D.
1173.

verge of ruin; from day to day all things grew worse.
The abbot's sole resource and means of relief was in
borrowing money, that so it might at least be possible
to maintain the dignity of his house. For eight
years before his death, there was never an Easter or
Michaelmas which did not see at least one or two
hundred pounds added to the debt. The bonds were
ever renewed, and the growing interest was converted
into principal.

This disease spread from the head to the members,
from the ruler to his subjects. So it came to pass
that if any official had a seal of his own, he also bound
himself in debt as he listed, both to Jews and Christians. Silken caps, and golden vessels, and the other
ornaments of the church, were often placed in pledge
without the assent of the monastery. I have seen a
bond made to William FitzIsabel for a thousand and
two score pounds, but know not the why nor wherefore. And I have seen another bond to Isaac, son of
Rabbi Joce, for four hundred pounds, but know not
wherefore it was made. I have seen also a third bond
to Benedict, the Jew of Norwich, for eight hundred
and fourscore pounds, and this was the origin and
cause of that debt.

Our buttery was destroyed, and the sacristan

William received it to restore whether he would or no. He secretly borrowed forty marks at interest from Benedict the Jew, and made him a bond, sealed with a certain seal which was wont to hang at the shrine of St. Edmund. With this the gilds and brotherhoods used to be sealed ; afterwards, but in no great haste, it was destroyed by order of the monastery. Now when that debt increased to one hundred pounds, the Jew came, bearing letters of the lord king concerning the sacristan's debt, and then at last that which had been hidden from the abbot and the monks appeared. So the abbot in anger would have deposed the sacristan, alleging a privilege of the lord pope that enabled him to remove Wiliam his sacristan when he would. However there came one to the abbot, who pleaded for the sacristan, and so won over the abbot that he suffered a bond to be made to Benedict the Jew for four hundred pounds, payable at the end of four years, that is, a bond for the hundred pounds to which the interest had increased, and for another hundred pounds which the same Jew had lent to the sacristan for the use of the abbot. And in full chapter the sacristan obtained that all this debt should be paid, and a bond was made and sealed with the seal of the monastery. For the abbot pretended that the debt was no concern of his, and did not affix his seal. However, at the end of the four years there was nothing wherewith the debt might be discharged, and a new bond was made for eight hundred and fourscore pounds, which was to be repaid at stated times, every year forescore pounds.

And the same Jew had many other bonds for smaller debts, and one bond which was for fourteen years, so that the sum of the debt owing to that Jew was a thousand and two hundred pounds, over and above the amount by which usury had increased it.

Then came the almoner of the lord king and told the lord abbot that many rumours concerning these great debts had come to the king. And when counsel had been taken with the prior and a few others, the almoner was brought into the chapter. Then, when we were seated and were silent, the abbot said: " Behold the almoner of the king, our lord and friend and yours, who, moved by love of God and Saint Edmund, has shown to us that the lord king has heard some evil report of us and you, and that the affairs of the church are ill-managed within and without the walls. And therefore I will, and command you upon your vow of obedience, that you say and make known openly how our affairs stand." So the prior arose, and speaking as it were one for all, said that the church was in good order, and that the rule was well and strictly kept within, and matters outside the walls carefully and discreetly managed; and that though we, like others round us, were slightly involved in debt, there was no debt which might give us cause for anxiety. When he heard this, the almoner said that he rejoiced greatly to hear this witness of the monastery, by which he meant these words of the prior. And the prior, and Master Geoffrey of Coutances, answered in these same words on another occasion, when they spoke in defence of the abbot at the time when Archbishop Richard, by virtue of his legatine power, came into our chapter, in the days before we possessed that exemption which we now enjoy.

Now I was then in my novitiate, and on a convenient occasion talked of these things to my master, who was teaching me the Rule, and in whose care I was placed; he was Master Samson, who was afterwards abbot. "What is this," I said, "that I hear? And why do you keep silence when you see and hear such things—you, who are a cloistered monk, and desire not offices, and fear God rather than man?" But he answered and said, "My son, the newly burnt child feareth the fire, and so it is with me and with many another. Prior Hugh has been lately deposed and sent into exile; Denis, and Hugo, and Roger de Hingham have but lately returned to the house from exile. I was in like manner imprisoned, and afterwards was sent to Acre, for that we spoke to the common good of our church against the will of the abbot. This is the hour of darkness; this is the hour in which flatterers triumph and are believed; their might is increased, nor can we prevail against them. These things must be endured for a while; the Lord see and judge!"

HOW THE MONASTERY WAS FREED FROM LEGATINE VISITATION

THERE came a rumour to Abbot Hugh that Richard, Archbishop of Canterbury, proposed to come and to hold a visitation of our church by virtue of his legatine authority. And A.D. 1176 having taken advice, the abbot sent to Rome and obtained exemption from the power of the said legate. But when the messenger returned to us from Rome, there was not found means of paying that which he had promised to the lord

pope and to the cardinals, unless in the circumstances use might be made of the cross which was
above the high altar, and of a Mary, and a John,
which images Archbishop Stigand had adorned with
much weight of gold and silver, and had given to the
blessed Edmund. Then some among our number,
who were very intimate with the abbot, said that the
very shrine of Saint Edmund itself ought to be
stripped in order to win so notable a privilege. But
they considered not the great danger that might
ensue from so great liberty. For if by chance we
should have an abbot who wished to waste the goods
of the church and evilly entreat his monastery, then
there would be no one to whom the monastery might
make complaint of the evil deeds of the abbot, who
would fear neither bishop, nor archbishop, nor legate,
and whose impunity would give him boldness in
wrongdoing.

CONCERNING MASTER DENIS THE CELLARER

Now in those days the cellarer, like the rest of
the officers of the monastery, borrowed money from
Jurnet the Jew, without the knowledge of the

monastery, on a bond sealed with the seal mentioned above. But when the debt had grown to three score pounds, the monastery was called upon to discharge the debt of the cellarer. He was desposed, though he defended himself by saying that for three years he, by command of the abbot, had received all guests in the guest-house, whether the abbot were at home or no, whom the abbot ought to have received according to the constitution of the house.

In his stead Master Dennis was appointed, and by his economy and care reduced that debt of sixty pounds to thirty. Towards the extinction of that debt we paid the thirty marks which Benedict de Blakeham gave to the monastery for the manors of Nowton and Whepstead. But the Jew's bond remains with the Jew to this day, and in it twenty-six pounds are written down as principal and for the debt of the cellarer.

On the third day after Master Dennis was made cellarer, three knights with their squires were brought into the guest-house to be entertained there, the abbot being at home and sitting in his chamber. Now when that great-hearted Achilles heard this, not wishing to fail in his office as did the others, he arose and took the keys of the cellar, and bearing the knights with him to the hall of the abbot, came himself into the abbot's presence. And he said to him, "Lord, you know well that the custom of the abbey is that knights and laymen be received in your hall, if the abbot be at home. I neither wish, nor am I able, to receive guests whose entertainment is your care. But if it be otherwise, take the keys of your cellar, and appoint another cellarer at your pleasure." When the abbot heard this, he received those knights perforce and ever after he received knights and laymen in accordance with ancient custom. And they are still so received when the abbot is at home.

HOW ABBOT HUGH STROVE TO WIN THE FAVOUR OF MASTER SAMSON

At one time Abbot Hugh desired to win the favour of Master Samson, and made him his subsacristan. He was often accused, often transferred from one office to another. For he was made guestmaster, and then pittance-master, then third prior and finally again subsacristan. Then many strove against him who afterwards were his flatterers. But Samson did not bear himself as did the other officials, nor could he ever be brought to flatter.

Wherefore the abbot said to his intimates that never had he seen a man whom he could not bend to his will, save Samson the subsacristan.

HOW ABBOT HUGH CAME BY HIS DEATH

In the twenty-third year of his being abbot, it came into the mind of Abbot Hugh to journey to the shrine of the blessed Thomas to pray there. And when he was almost at his journey's end, and was near unto Rochester on the morrow of the Nativity of the Blessed Mary, he most unhappily fell, so that his knee-pan was put out and lodged in the ham of his leg. Physicians hastened to him, and put him to pain in many ways, but they healed him not. So he was borne back to us in a horse-litter, and received with great concern, as was fitting. To put it shortly, his leg mortified and the sickness spread to his heart. Pain brought on a tertian fever, and in the fourth fit he died, rendering his soul to God on the morrow of St. Brice's day.

A.D. 1180.
9TH SEPTEMBER.

Ere he was dead, all things were thrown into disorder by his servants, so that in the abbot's houses there was nothing at all left, except stools and tables which could not be carried away. There hardly remained to the abbot a coverlet and quilts which were old and torn, and which someone who had taken away those which were sound, had left in their place. There was not even some thing of a penny's value which might be given to the poor for the good of his soul. The sacristan said that it was not his affair to do this, declaring that he had found the money for the expenses of the abbot and his household for a full month, since neither would those who farmed the townships pay anything before the appointed time, nor would the creditors give any grace, as they saw the abbot to be sick unto death. However the tenant of Palegrave found fifty shillings for distribution to the poor, because he entered upon his tenancy of Palegrave on that day. But those fifty shillings were afterwards again paid to the king's officers, who exacted the full rent for the use of the king.

HOW THE DEATH OF ABBOT HUGH WAS TOLD TO THE KING, AND OF THOSE THINGS WHICH THE SERVANTS OF THE KING DID

WHEN Abbot Hugh had been laid to rest, it was decreed in the chapter that one should tell the death of the abbot to Ranulf de Glanvill, Justiciar of

England. Master Samson and Master Robert Ruffus hastened across the sea, bearing this same news to the lord King, and obtained from him letters directing that the possessions and revenues of the monastery, which were distinct from those of the abbot, should remain entirely in the hands of the prior and of the monastery, and that the rest of the abbey's property should be in the hands of the King. The wardship of the abbey was given to Robert de Cokefield and to Robert de Flamvill the senschal, who at once placed under surety and pledges those of the servants and relatives of the abbot to whom the abbot had given anything after he fell ill, or who had taken anything from the property of the abbot. And they also treated the chaplain of the abbot in the same way, for whom the prior became surety. And entering our vestry, they made a double inventory of the ornaments of the church.

HOW THE PRIOR RULED THE MONASTERY, WHILE THERE WAS NO ABBOT

THERE being no abbot, the prior took care, above all things, to preserve peace in the monastery and to maintain the repute of the house in the matter of receiving guests. He wished to disturb no one,

to provoke to no one to anger, that he might keep all
men and all things in quiet. But he overlooked
some acts of our officials which should have been
corrected; and especially in the case of the sacristan,
as if he cared not how that office was performed.
Now the sacristan, while the abbey was vacant, neither
paid any debt nor erected any building, but the offerings and accidental receipts were foolishly wasted.
Wherefore the prior, who was head of the monastery,
seemed to many to be blameworthy, and was called
slack. And our brothers reminded each other of this
when the time came for electing an abbot.

HOW THE CELLARER AND THE SACRIS-
TAN BEHAVED DURING THE VACANCY

OUR cellarer entertained all guests of whatever condition, at the expense of the monastery. William the
sacristan, for his part gave and spent. Kind man! he
spent indiscriminately, and blinded the eyes of all
with gifts.

CONCERNING THE CONDUCT OF SAMSON
THE SUBSACRISTAN DURING THE
VACANCY

SAMSON the subsacristan, who was master over the
workmen, did his utmost that nothing which was

broken, and no chink or crack, should remain un-repaired. In this way he won the favour of the monastery, and more especially of the cloistered monks. At that time, and under Samson's direction, was our choir built. He determined the subjects of the paintings, and composed elegiac verses for them. He made a great store of stone and sand for building the great tower of the church. And when he was asked where he found the money for this work, he answered that some of the townsfolk had given him money secretly for the building and completing of the tower. But some of our brothers said that Warin our monk and custodian of the shrine, had agreed to take, or as it were to steal, some part of the offerings of the shrine, and to spend it for the necessary pur-poses of the church, especially for the building of the tower. They were led to this opinion by the fact that they saw the strange uses to which these offerings were put by others, who, to speak the truth, did steal them. And in order to remove from themselves the suspicion of so happy a theft, Samson and Warin made a hollow chest, in the middle of the cover of which there was a hole, and which was secured with an iron bar. This chest they caused to be placed in the great church near the door outside the choir, where all the

people passed by, that men might place therein gifts
for the building of the tower.

HOW THE ENEMIES OF SAMSON PRE-VAILED AGAINST HIM, BUT ONLY FOR A TIME

But William the sacristan mistrusted his colleague
Samson, as did many others, both Christians and Jews,
who favoured the opinion of the same William. The
Jews, I say, to whom the sacristan was said to be a
father and a patron. And they did rejoice in his
protection, having freedom to enter and to leave the
monastery, and wandering all over it. For they
walked by the altars and round the shrine while high
mass was being celebrated; their money was lodged in
our treasury under the care of the sacristan; and, a
thing still more foolish, their wives and little ones
were entertained in our pittancy during time of war.

Therefore, having taken counsel together how they
might attack Samson, his enemies and adversaries went
to Robert de Cokefield and to his colleague, who had
the wardship of the abbey, and persuaded them to
forbid in the name of the king that any one should do
any work or build anything while the abbacy was

vacant, but rather should the money from the offerings be collected and saved for the payment of some part of the debt. Thus was Samson mocked, and his strength went from him, and he could not from that time do any work as he desired. But though his enemies could delay his work, they could not finally interrupt it. For he regained his strength and over-threw the two middle pillars, that is, he removed the two wardens in whom the malice of the others trusted. And afterwards in course of time, the Lord gave him power to perform his vow that he would build the said tower, and to finish it according to his wish. And so it came to pass as though a voice from Heaven had said to him, "Well done, thou good and faithful servant; thou hast been faithful over a few things; I will make thee ruler over many things."

HOW THE MONKS DISPUTED AMONG THEMSELVES WHICH OF THEM SHOULD BE ABBOT

THE abbacy being vacant, we often, as was right, made supplications unto the Lord and to the blessed martyr Edmund that they would give us and our church a fit pastor. Three times in each week, after leaving the chapter, did we prostrate ourselves in the choir and sing seven penitential psalms. And there were some who would not have been so earnest in their prayers if they had known who was to become abbot. As to the choice of an abbot, if the king should grant us free election, there was much difference of opinion, some of it openly expressed, some of it privately ; and every man had his own ideas.

One said of a certain brother, "He, that brother is a good monk, a likely person. He knows much of the rule and of the customs of the church. It is true that he is not so profoundly wise as are some others, but he is quite capable of being abbot. Abbot Ording was illiterate, and yet he was a good abbot and ruled this house wisely ; and one reads in the fable that the frogs did better to elect a log to be their king than a serpent, who hissed venomously, and when he had hissed, devoured his subjects." Another answered, " How could this thing be ? How could one who does not know letters preach in the chapter, or to the people on feast days ? How could one who does not know the scriptures have the knowledge of binding and loosing ? For the rule of souls is the art of arts, the highest form of knowledge. God forbid that a dumb idol be set up in the church of Saint Edmund, where many men are to be found who are learned and industrious."

Again, one said of another, " That brother is a literate man, eloquent and prudent, and strict in his observance of the rule.   He loves the monastery greatly, and has suffered many ills for the good of the church.   He is worthy to be made abbot."   Another answered, " From good clerks deliver us, oh Lord ! That it may please Thee to preserve us from the cheats of Norfolk ; we beseech Thee to hear us ! "

And again, one said of one, " That brother is a good husbandman ; this is proved by the state of his office, and from the posts in which he has served well, and from the buildings and repairs which he has effected.   He is well able to work and to defend the house, and he is something of a scholar, though too much learning has not made him mad.   He is worthy of the abbacy."   Another answered, " God forbid that a man who can neither read nor sing, nor celebrate the holy office, a man who is dishonest and unjust, and who evil intreats the poor men, should be made abbot."

Again, one said of another, " That brother is a kindly man, friendly and amiable, peaceful and calm, generous and liberal, a learned and eloquent man, and proper enough in face and gait. He is beloved of many within and without the walls, and such an one might become abbot to the great honour of the church, if God wills." Another answered, "It is no credit, but rather a disgrace, in a man to be too particular as to what he eats and drinks, to think it a virtue to sleep much, to know well how to spend and to know little how to gain, to snore while others keep vigil, to wish ever to have abundance, and not to trouble when debts daily increase, or when money spent brings no return; to be one who hates anxiety and toil, caring nothing while one day passes and another dawns; to be one who loves and cherishes flatterers and liars; to be one man in word and another in deed. From such a prelate the Lord defend us."

And again, one said of his friend, "That man is almost wiser than all of us, and that both in secular and in ecclesiastical matters. He is a man skilled in counsel, strict in the rule, learned and eloquent, and noble in stature; such a prelate would become our church." Another answered, "That would be true, if he were a man of good and approved repute. But his character has been questioned, perhaps falsely, perhaps rightly. And though the man is wise, humble in the chapter devoted to the singing of psalms, strict in his conduct in the cloister while he is a cloistered monk, this is only from force of habit. For if he have authority in any office, he is too scornful, holding monks of no account, and being on familiar terms with secular men, and if he be angry, he will scarce say a word willingly to any brother, even in answer to a question."

I heard in truth another brother abused by some because he had an impediment in his speech, and it was said of him that he had pastry or draff in his mouth when he should have spoken. And I myself, as I was then young, understood as a child, spake as a child; and I said that I would not consent that any one should be made abbot unless he knew something of dialectic, and knew how to distinguish the true from the false. One, moreover, who was wise in his own eyes, said, "May Almighty God give us a foolish and stupid pastor, that he may be driven to use our help." And I heard, forsooth, that one man who was industrious, learned, and pre-eminent for his high birth, was abused by some of the older men because he was a novice. The novices said of their elders that they were invalid old men, and little capable of ruling an abbey. And so many men said many things, and every man was fully persuaded in his own mind.

HOW SAMSON THE SUBSACRISTAN BORE HIMSELF WHILE OTHERS DISCUSSED THE VACANCY

THEN I saw Samson the subsacristan sitting by, for the time of this little council was a season of blood-letting, when the cloistered monks were wont to reveal the secrets of their hearts in turn, and to discuss matters one with another. I saw him sitting by and laughing to himself, while he kept silence and marked that which each one said, so that at the end of twenty years he was able to remember some part of the various opinions which I have set forth above.

HOW THE AUTHOR SPOKE HIS MIND TOO HASTILY

AND when I heard these things, I was wont to answer to those who so judged, and to say that if we had to wait to choose an abbot until we found one without spot or flaw, we should never find such a one, since there is none living without fault, and nothing altogether good. At one time I could not refrain my spirit, but put forward my own opinion only too readily, thinking that I was speaking to faithful ears.   And I said that one was not worthy of the abbacy who had before loved me dearly and done much good to me.   And I put forward another as worthy and named him, a man whom I loved but little.   I spoke according to my conscience, thinking rather of the general well-being of the church than of my own promotion ; and I spoke the truth, as subsequent events proved.   And behold, one of the sons of Belial revealed my saying to my benefactor and friend, wherefore to this very day I have never been able, by prayer or present, to regain his full favour.   What I have said, I have said.   And the word once uttered flies beyond recall.

One thing remains for me,—that I take care henceforth ; and if I should live long enough to see the abbey once more vacant, I will see what, and to whom and when I speak of so weighty a matter, that I offend not God by lying or man by hasty talk.   Then it will be my care, if I live, that we elect one who is neither a very good monk, not a very wise clerk, nor too foolish, nor too dissolute ; lest, if he know too much, he have also too much confidence in himself and in his own opinion, and hold others of small account ; or if he be too foolish, he be abused by others.   I know that one has said, " You will walk most safely in the middle," and that "Blessed are those who steer a middle course." And perchance it is wiser counsel to be silent altogether, so that I say in my heart, "He that is able to receive it, let him receive it."

HOW THE ARCHBISHOP OF NORWAY DWELT IN THE ABBOT'S LODGINGS WHILE THE ABBACY WAS VACANT

WHILE the abbacy was vacant, Augustine, Archbishop of Norway, dwelt with us in the abbot's lodgings, and by command of the king received ten shillings every day from the revenues of the abbot. He assisted us greatly to gain freedom of election, bearing witness of the good, and publicly declaring in the presence of the king that which he had seen and heard.

A.D. 1181.

OF THE MARTYRDOM OF SAINT ROBERT

IN those days was the holy child Robert martyred, and was buried in our church. And many signs and wonders were wrought among the people, as we have related in another place.

A.D. 1181. 10TH JUNE.

HOW THIRTEEN MEN WERE CHOSEN, BY COMMAND OF THE KING, TO ELECT AN ABBOT IN THE PRESENCE OF THE KING

Now when a year and three months had passed since the death of Abbot Hugh, the lord king com-

A.D. 1182.
FEBRUARY.

manded by his letters that our prior and twelve members of the monastery, by whose lips the opinion of the whole community might be expressed unanimously, should appear before him on a stated day to elect an abbot.

On the morrow after receiving the letters, we gathered in the chapter for the purpose of performing so important a task. And first the letters of the lord king were read in the assembly of the monastery; then we offered prayers, and bound the prior on the peril of his soul that he should conscientiously nominate to go with him twelve men, from whose life and manners he knew well that they would not stray from the right path.

Then he, by inspiration of the Holy Spirit, gave ear to these prayers, and named six from one side of the choir and six from the other, and he gave us satisfaction without any dispute arising. From the right-hand side of the choir he named Geoffrey de Fordham, Benedict, Master Dennis, Master Samson the sub-sacristan, Hugh the third prior, and Master Hermer, who was then a novice.   From the left side he named William the sacristan, Andrew, Peter de Broc, Roger the cellarer, Master Ambrose, and Master Walter the physician.

But one said, "What shall be done if these thirteen cannot agree on the choice of an abbot in the presence of the king?"   One answered, "That would be a perpetual shame to us and our church."   For that cause many wished that the election might be made at home before the departure of the rest, so that by this means there might be no dissension in the presence of the king.   But it seemed to us foolish and unbecoming to do this without the royal assent, since as yet we had no certain knowledge that we should obtain freedom of election from the lord king.

HOW SAMSON SUGGESTED THAT THE MONASTERY SHOULD APPOINT MEN TO MAKE A SECRET CHOICE OF AN ABBOT, AND HOW THIS WAS DONE

THEN Samson the subsacristan, speaking by the Spirit of God, said, "Let a middle course be taken, that so danger may be avoided on either side. Let four confessors be chosen from the monastery and two of the older priors, men of repute, and let them look upon and take in their hands the most holy gospels, and choose among themselves three members of the monastery, men specially fitted according to the rule of the holy Benedict for this purpose. Then let them write down the names and seal that which is written, and let them give the writing thus secured to us on the eve of our departure for the court. And when we are come to the court, if it shall be determined that we have free election, then and not till then let the seal be broken, and so shall we know certainly the three who must be named in the presence of the king. Let it also be resolved that if the lord king will not grant us one of our own number, then the writing shall be brought back, with the seal unbroken, and delivered to the six sworn men, that so their secret may remain a secret for ever on the peril of their souls."

In this council we all agreed, and the four confessors were nominated, to wit, Eustace, Gilbert de Alueth, Hugh the third prior, and Anthony, with two other old men, Thurstan and Rualdus. And when this had been done, we went out chanting the "Verba mea," while the said six remained behind with the rule of

St. Benedict in their hands, and completed the matter as had been ordained.

While these six men performed their work, we had various opinions as to the choice of different men, but all considered it to be certain that Samson would be one of them. For they called to mind his labours and the danger of death, which he had endured in his journey to Rome for the good of our church, and how he had been ill treated, and bound, and put in prison by Abbot Hugh, because he spoke to the common advantage. And they considered he was a man who could not be brought to flatter, though he might be driven to keep silence.

So, after some delay, the whole monastery was summoned to return to the chapter. And the old men said that they had done as had been commanded them.

HOW, ON THE ADVICE OF SAMSON, IT WAS DECIDED WHAT SHOULD BE DONE IF THE KING WOULD NOT GRANT FREEDOM OF ELECTION

THEN the prior asked what and if the lord king would not accept any one of the three whose names were written down. And it was answered that, since whomsoever the king wished to be received, must be received, there was but one course open to our church It was added also that if those thirteen brothers should see in any writing aught that should be altered, they should make the alteration, according to God, unanimously and after consultation.

Samson the subsacristan, sitting at the feet of the prior, said " It would be for the good of the church were all to swear on the word of truth that on whomsoever the lot of election shall fall, that man shall treat the monastery reasonably, and not change the chief officials without the assent of the house, nor burden the sacristan, nor make any one a monk without the consent of the monastery." And we agreed on this matter, all raising their right hands in token of their approval. And it was provided that if the lord king willed that some stranger should be made abbot, the thirteen should not accept this man save with the advice of the brothers who remained at home.

HOW THE CHOSEN THIRTEEN JOURNEYED TO THE KING

On the morrow, therefore, these thirteen set out for the court. Last of all was Samson, who had charge of the expenses of the journey as being subsacristan. And he bore a letter-case round his neck, in which were contained the letters of the monastery, as if he were only servant of them all. So, with no attendant, and with his frock borne in his arms, he went out of the court, and followed far behind his comrades.

On their journey to the court, the brothers gathered together, and Samson said that it would be well if all were to swear that whoever might be made abbot, should restore the churches on the demense lands of the monastery to the exercise of hospitality. To this all agreed save the prior, and he said, "We have sworn enough; you will so limit the power of the abbot, that I would not care to be abbot at all." And for this reason, they did not swear; and it was well that they did not do, for had this oath been taken it would not have been observed.

OF THE DREAMS WHICH THE BROTHERS DREAMED CONCERNING THE ELECTION OF A NEW ABBOT

THEN on the day on which the thirteen departed, while we were sitting in the cloister, William de Hastings, one of our brothers, said, "I know that we shall have one of our own number as abbot." And when he was asked how he knew this, he answered that he had beheld in dreams a prophet, clothed in white, standing before the gates of the monastery. Him he had asked in the name of the Lord whether we should have one of ourselves as abbot. And the prophet answered, " Ye shall have one of your own number, but he shall raven as a wolf among you." And this dream was partly fulfilled, since he that became abbot strove rather to be feared than loved, as many were wont to say.

Another brother also, Edmund by name, was sitting by, and declared that Samson would be abbot, relating a dream which he had seen on the previous night. For he said that he had seen in dreams Roger the cellarer and Hugh the third prior standing before the altar, and Samson in their midst, head and shoulders taller than they, and wearing a long and flowing cloak, fastened at his shoulders, and he was standing as it were like a champion about to engage in a duel. Then the holy Edmund arose from his shrine—as it seemed to the brother in his dream—and showed his feet and legs bare, as though sickness was upon him. Then when one rose and would have covered the feet of the saint, the saint said, " Come not near. Lo ! he shall cover my feet," and pointed his finger towards Samson. This is the interpretation of the dream : In that a champion was seen, this signified that he who was to become abbot would be constant in labour, alike when disputing with the archbishop of Canterbury about the pleas of the crown, and when striving with the knights of St. Edmund for the full payment of scutages, or with the burghers about encroachments on the market, or with the sokemen for the suits of hundreds; and that he was as it were a champion anxious to overcome his enemies by fighting, that so far as in him lay he might recover the rights and liberties of his church. Moreover, he covered the feet of the holy martyr, when he completed fully the towers of the church which had been begun a hundred years before.

Such dreams did our brothers dream, and at once told them first of all in the cloister and then in the court. And so it came to pass that before vespers the people openly said that this and this and this man was elected, and that one of them would be abbot.

HOW THE THIRTEEN CAME TO THE KING AND SHOWED TO HIM THE NAMES OF THOSE WHOM THE CONFESSORS HAD SELECTED

So the prior and the twelve with him, after many labours stood at last in the presence of the king at

Waltham, a manor of the bishop of
Winchester, on the second Sunday in
Lent.   And the lord king received
them graciously, and declared that he wished to act
according to the will of God and for the honour of
our church.   Then he gave command to the brothers
through his proctors, Richard bishop of Winchester
and Geoffrey the chancellor, who was afterwards
archbishop of York, that they should nominate three
members of our monastery.

A.D. 1182.
21ST FEBRUARY.

Then the prior and the brothers withdrew themselves, as it were to discuss this matter, and drew forth
the seal and broke it, and found these names written
down in this order,—Samson, the sub-sacristan, Roger
the cellarer, and Hugh the third prior.   And at this
the brothers who were of greater dignity blushed.
Moreover all marvelled that the same Hugh should
be both an elector and one of the elected.   But
because they could not alter the thing they unanimously changed the order of the names, naming
Hugh, because he was third prior, first, and Roger
the cellarer next, and Samson third.   Thus, as far as
words went, they made the last first, and the first last.

But the king, having first asked whether they were
born in his land, and in whose lordship, said that he

did not know them, and commanded that they should name three other members of the monastery with them.

HOW THE THIRTEEN, BY COMMAND OF THE KING, CHOSE THREE OTHER NAMES FROM THE MONASTERY, AND THREE STRANGERS

AND when this had been granted, William the sacristan said, "Our prior ought to be nominated, for he is our head," and this was readily agreed. Then the prior said, "William the sacristan is a good man." The same was said of Dennis, and was agreed. And when these were named in the presence of the king without any delay, the king marvelled, saying, "These men act quickly. God is with them."

And after that the king commanded that for the honour of the kingdom, they should nominate three persons from other houses. When they heard this the brothers feared, for they suspected a fraud. Yet did they agree to nominate three, but under conditions, namely, that they would receive no one save with the assent of the members of the monastery who were at home. And they named three, master Nicholas de Waringford, who was afterwards for a

while abbot of Malmesbury, and Bertrand, prior of
St. Faith's, who was afterwards abbot of Chertsey,
and lord H. de St. Neots, a Monk of Bec, a most
pious man, and in both secular and spiritual matters
very prudent.

HOW THE LIST OF NAMES WAS REDUCED FROM NINE TO TWO

When this had been done, the king sent them thanks
and commanded that three of the nine should be removed, and the three strangers were at once removed,
that is, the prior of St. Faith's, who was afterwards
abbot of Chertsey, and Nicholas, the monk of St.
Alban's, who was afterwards abbot of Malmesbury,
and the prior of St. Neot's.

William the sacristan of his accord withdrew, two
of the five were removed by the order of the king, and
finally one of the last three, so that there remained
then two, namely, the prior and Samson.

HOW SAMSON WAS ELECTED ABBOT

Then at last the above-mentioned proctors of the
lord king were summoned to the council of the brothers.
And Dennis, speaking as one for all, began to commend
the persons of the prior and Samson.   He said that

they were both learned men, both good, both praise-worthy in their lives and of unblemished reputation. But even at the climax of his speech he put forward Samson, multiplying words in his praise, saying that he was a man strict in his conduct, stern in correcting faults, apt for labour, prudent in temporal matters, and proved in divers offices.

Then the bishop of Winchester answered, "We know well what you would say, from your words we gather that your prior has appeared to you to be some-what slack, and that you wish to have him who is called Samson." Dennis answered, "Both of them are good men, but we desire to have the better, if God wills." Thereupon the bishop said, "Of two good things, the greater good should be selected. Say openly, do you desire to have Samson?" And many, and they a majority, answered plainly, "We wish to have Samson," and none spoke against him. Some, however, were silent from caution, wishing to offend neither candidate.

Then Samson was nominated in the presence of the lord king, and when the king had consulted with his men for a while, all were summoned. And the king said, "You have presented to me Samson. I know him not. If you had presented your prior to me, I would have accepted him, for I have seen and know him. But I will only do what you will. Take heed to yourselves; by the true eyes of God, if you do ill, I will exact a recompense at your hands."

Then he asked the prior if he assented to the choice and wished it, and the prior answered that he did will it, and that Samson was worthy of much greater honour. Therefore he was elected, and fell at the king's feet and embraced them. Then he arose quickly and hastened to the altar, with his head erect and without changing his expression, chanting the "Miserere mei, Deus" with the brothers.

And when the king saw this, he said to those that stood by, "By the eyes of God, this elect thinks that he is worthy to rule the abbey."

HOW THE NEWS OF THE ELECTION CAME TO THE MONASTERY AND HOW SAMSON WAS BLESSED

THE news of this election came to the monastery, and all the cloistered monks or almost all of them were rejoiced, and also some of the officials, but few. "It is well," said many, "because it is well." Others said that this was not so, "Of a truth, we have all been bewitched."

Before he returned to us, the elect received his benediction from the lord of Winchester, who in the same hour in the which he placed the mitre on the abbot's head and the ring on his finger, said, "This man is worthy of the abbacy of St. Edmund, and for a long while have I known it.

A.D. 1182
28TH FEBRUARY.

Therefore the abbot retained with him three monks, and allowed the rest to return home. And he announced that he would himself come on Palm Sunday, and charged certain men with the care of providing those things which might be necessary for his feast.

HOW SAMSON, HAVING BEEN MADE ABBOT, RETURNED AND WAS RECEIVED AT THE MONASTERY

On his homeward way a multitude of new relations met him, desiring to serve him. But he answered all of them that he was content with the servants of the prior, and that he was unable to maintain others until he had consulted the monastery on the matter. But one knight he did retain, a man who was eloquent and skilled in the law. This he did not only from consideration of their relationship, but from arguments of utility also, as he was indeed used to secular affairs. He received him as a novice and as his assessor in temporal disputes. For he was a new abbot and unskilful in such matters, as he himself protested, since until he received the abbacy he had never held any office in which surety and pledge was given.

On Palm Sunday he was received with due honour and with ceremony also by his monastery.

Now the lord abbot was thus received. The night before he had laid at Kentford, and at the proper moment we went to meet him in solemn procession, after leaving the chapter, as far as the gate of the grave-yard, while bells were rung in the choir and outside it. But he was surrounded by a multitude of men, and when he saw the monastery, dismounted from his horse without the threshold of the gate, and causing his sandals to be removed, was received within the door barefooted, the prior and the sacristan supporting him on either side. And we chanted the responses "Benedictus Dominus" from the service for Trinity Sunday, and afterwards the "Martiri adhuc" from that for St. Edmund, and conducted the abbot as far as the high altar.

A.D. 1182.
21ST MARCH.

And when this had been done, the organs and bells were silenced, and the prior said the prayer "Omnipotens sempiterne Deus, miserere huic," over the prostrate abbot. Then the abbot made oblation and kissed the shrine, and returned to the choir. There Samson the precentor took him by the hand and led him to the abbot's chair on the western side of the choir, and while he stood there the precentor at once began "Te Deum laudamus," and while it was being chanted, the abbot was embraced by the prior and by the whole monastery.

And so, these ceremonies being completed, the abbot entered the chapter, the whole monastery and many others following. He said many times "Benedicite," and then he first returned thanks to the monastery that they had chosen him, the least of them all, as he said, not for his own merits but only by the will of God, to be their lord and pastor. And asking in a few words that they would pray for him, he addressed the clerks and knights, and asked them to advise him for the good of the monastery.

Then Wimer, the sheriff, answered for them all, and said, "We also are ready to be with you in counsel and in helping you in every way, as with a dear lord whom the Lord has called for His honour, and for the honour of the holy martyr Edmund."

Afterwards the charters of the king concerning the donation of the abbacy were brought forth, and were read in the hearing of all. The abbot himself also prayed that God would guide him according to His grace, and all answered "Amen." Then he went into his own chamber, and celebrated his day of festival with more than a thousand guests and with great joy.

HOW ABBOT SAMSON BEGAN TO RULE THE MONASTERY

In those days I was prior's chaplain, and within four months was made chaplain to the abbot. And I noted many things and committed them to memory. So, on the morrow of his feast, the abbot assembled the prior and some few others together, as if to seek advice from others, but he himself knew what he would do.

He said that a new seal must be made and adorned with a mitred effigy of himself, though his predecessors had not had such a seal. For a time, however, he used the seal of our prior, writing at the end of all letters that he did so for the time being because he had no seal of his own. And afterwards he ordered his household, and transferred various officials to other offices, saying that he proposed to maintain twenty-six horses in his court, and many times he declared that "a child

must first crawl, and afterwards he may stand upright
and walk." And he laid this special command upon
his servants, that they should take care that he might
not be laid open to the charge of not providing enough
food and drink, but that they should assiduously provide for the maintenance of the hospitality of the
house.

In these matters, and in all the things which he did
and determined, he trusted fully in the help of God
and his own good sense, holding it to be shameful to
rely upon the counsel of another, and thinking he was
sufficient unto himself. The monks marvelled and
the knights were angered; they blamed his pride, and
often defamed him at the court of the king, saying
that he would not act in accordance with the advice
of his freemen. He himself put away from his privy
council all the great men of the abbey, both lay and
literate, men without whose advice and assistance it
seemed impossible that the abbey could be ruled. For
this reason Ranulf de Glanville, justiciar of England,
was at first offended with him, and was less well-dis-
posed towards him than was expedient, until he knew
well from definite proofs that the abbot acted providently and prudently, both in domestic and in external
affairs.

HOW THE ABBOT MET THE DEMAND OF THOMAS DE HASTINGS THAT HIS NEPHEW SHOULD BE STEWARD

A GENERAL summons was sent out, and on the fourth day of Easter all the barons, and knights, and freemen came to do homage. And, lo! Thomas de Hastings came also with a great multitude of knights, and brought with him Henry his nephew, who was not yet a knight, and for whom he demanded the office of steward with the customary dues thereof, as his charter provided. And to this demand the abbot at once answered, "I neither deny, nor wish to deny, his right to Henry. If he were able to serve me in his own person, I would grant him the means of supporting ten men and eight horses in my court. And if you will present a steward to me, who knows how to fulfil the office of steward and is able to do so, I will receive him on the same terms as my predecessor had his steward on the day whereon he was alive and dead, that is, I will allow him four horses with the things needful for them. But if you will not agree to this, I will make complaint before the king and before the chief justiciar."

When the abbot had so spoken, the matter was

A.D. 1182. 1st APRIL.

postponed. But afterwards a certain simple and foolish steward, by name Gilbert, was presented to him, and before he received him, the abbot said to his intimates, "If the ignorance of the steward leads to the ill-rendering of the justice of the king, then it will be he who will be responsible to the king and not I, for he gained the stewardship by hereditary right. For the time, therefore, I would rather accept him than another, even more incompetent, to my loss. By God's help, I will be my own steward."

HOW THE ABBOT DEALT WITH THE LANDS OF HIS HOUSE

WHEN homage had been received, the abbot demanded an aid from the knights, and they promised twenty shillings from each fee of a knight. But they at once took counsel, and reduced the aid by twelve pounds from twelve knights, alleging that these twelve ought to assist the other forty to keep ward, and to make scutages, and also in assisting the abbey. When the abbot heard this, he was wroth, and said to his friends that should his life be spared, he would repay them like for like, and injury for injury.

After this, the abbot caused inquest to be made in every manor belonging to the abbacy as to the annual revenues of the free men, and the names of the villeins, and their holdings, and the services due from each, and caused all these details to be written down. Then he restored the old halls and ruined houses, through which kites and crows flew; he built new chapels, and rooms and seats in many places where there had never been buildings, save perhaps barns.

He also made many parks, which he filled with beasts, and had a huntsman and dogs. And whenever any important guest arrived, he used to sit with his monks in some retired grove, and watch the coursing for a while; but I never saw him interested in hunting.

He made many clearings and brought land into cultivation, in everything regarding the advantage of the abbacy. But would that he had watched with equal care over the grants of the manors of the monastery. For he received our manors of Bradfield and Rougham for a while into his own hand, making good the loss of rent by the expenditure of forty pounds, which he afterwards handed over to us when he heard that the monastery murmured because he held our manors in his own hands.

For the management of the same manors and for the management of all other affairs, he appointed monks and laymen who were wiser than those who had previously held the posts, and who made careful provision for us and our lands.

Then he received eight hundreds into his own hands, and when Robert de Cokefield died, he took the hundred of Cosford. All these he handed over to the care of the servants of his own table. Matters of greater moment were kept for his own decision, and those which were of less import were decided by his agents; all things he turned to his advantage.

By his command, a general account was drawn up for every hundred of the leets and suits, of the hidages and customary supplies of fodder, of the hens which ought to be paid to him, and of all the other customary dues, revenues, and expenses, which the tenants had always concealed to a great extent. All these things he reduced to writing, so that within four years of his election, no one could deceive him as to the resources of the abbey even to a penny's value, whereas he had received nothing in writing from his predecessors concerning the management of the abbey, except a little schedule containing the names of the knights of St. Edmund and the names of the manors, and the rent which attached to each farm. Now he called this book of his, his Calendar, in the which also were written down all the debts which he had paid. And he consulted this book almost daily, as if in it he saw the image of his probity as in a glass.

OF THAT WHICH WAS DONE AT THE ABBOT'S FIRST CHAPTER

On the first day on the which he held a chapter, he confirmed to us under his new seal the sixty shillings for Southrey, which his predecessors had in the first instance unjustly received from Edmund, called the golden monk, that the same might hold the said township to farm all the days of his life.

And he proposed an edict that no one should pledge the ornaments of the church henceforth without the assent of the monastery, as had been done formerly. He proposed also that no charter should be sealed with the seal of the monastery save in the chapter and in the presence of the whole community.

Then he made Hugh subsacristan, ordaining that William the sacristan should do nothing in the office of sacristan, either as to receipts or as to expenses, save by his assent. Afterwards, but on the same day, he removed the former custodians of the oblations to other offices. And last of all he deposed William himself, whereupon certain who loved William said,

"See the abbot! See the wolf of whom one dreamed! See how he ravens!"

HOW CERTAIN MEN WISHED TO CONSPIRE AGAINST THE ABBOT

THEN some wished to conspire against the abbot. And when this was revealed to the abbot, as he wished neither to keep silence altogether, nor to disturb the monastery, he entered the chapter on the morrow. And there he drew forth a small bag full of cancelled bonds, to which the seals were still attached, some of which were those of his predecessor, some of the prior, some of the sacristan, some of the chamberlain, and some of other officials. Of these the total was three thousand two score and twelve pounds, and one pure mark, over and above the increase due to usury, the amount of which none could know; and for all these he had made some arrangement within a year of his election, and within twelve years he had paid them in full.

And he said, "Observe the wisdom of our sacristan, William! See the number of bonds marked with his seal, in which he has pledged silken caps, dalmatics, silver vases, and books of the gospels bound in gold, without the assent of the monastery. And all these things I have settled and restored to you." And he added many other words, showing wherefore he had deposed William. But on the principal cause he kept silence, not wishing to make him a public example.

And all things became peaceful once more when he had replaced William with the precentor Samson, who was a man pleasing to all of us, and well known to be without fault. But the abbot ordered that the houses of the sacristan in the graveyard should be utterly destroyed, as if they were unworthy to stand above ground. And for this the cause was the frequent drinking bouts and certain things which cannot be mentioned, which he had seen when he was subsacristan with sorrow and pain. So he caused all the buildings to be levelled with the ground, and within a year, where there had stood a noble building we saw beans growing, and where casks of wine had lain we saw nettles in abundance.

HOW THE ABBOT JOURNEYED THROUGH THE LANDS OF SAINT EDMUND, AND HOW HE ESCAPED DEATH AT WARKTON

AFTER the end of Easter the abbot went through all his manors and ours, and through those which we had confirmed in fee to tenants. And from all and sundry he demanded an aid and recognition, according to the custom of the realm. Daily he grew skilled in earthly learning and turned his attention to the acquisition of knowledge of external affairs and of providing for them.

But when he was come to Warkton and was at night sleeping, a voice came to him saying, " Samson, arise up quickly," and again, " Rise, thou tarriest too long." So he arose half dazed, and looking round about him saw in a necessary place a light, a candle which Reiner the monk had left there through carelessness, and which was about to fall on the straw. And when the abbot had put it out, he went through the house and found the door—for there was but one —so fastened that it could only be opened with a key, and the windows barred. Wherefore, had the fire grown, both he and all they who were sleeping in that building would have perished. For there was no way by which they might have gone out or escaped.

HOW THE CREDITORS OF THE ABBEY DEMANDED PAYMENT, AND HOW THE ABBOT TOOK HIS MANORS INTO HIS OWN HAND

Now at that time, wheresoever the abbot went, there hastened to him both Jews and Christians demanding payment of the debts due to them. And they so disturbed the abbot, and caused him such anxiety, that he lost his sleep, and grew pale and thin. Then he said, "There will be no rest for my soul until I shall see an end of my indebtedness."

When Michaelmas came, he took all his manors into his hand, with very few necessary implements and but little stock. He forgave Walter de Hatfield nineteen pounds of arrears of rent, in return for receiving from him the four manors in the which he had been confirmed as tenant by abbot Hugh, namely, Hargrave, Saxham, Chevington and Stapleford.

HOW THE ABBOT DID NOT THEN TAKE HARLOW INTO HIS OWN HAND

But the abbot delayed to receive Harlow, and for this cause. It chanced that once when we were returning from London through the forest, that in the hearing of the lord abbot I asked an old woman who passed us whose this wood was, and to what township it belonged, and who was its lord or who was warden over it. And she answered that it was a wood of the abbot of St. Edmund, of the township of Harlow, and that one called Arnald was warden of it.

And when I asked concerning him as to how he bore himself towards the men of the township, she answered that he had been a fiend incarnate, an enemy of God, and one who evil-intreated the poor. But now, she said, he fears the new abbot of St. Edmund, whom he believes to be wise and provident, and therefore treats his men well. And when he heard this the abbot was rejoiced, and delayed for a season to take that manor into his own hand.

HOW THE ABBOT MANAGED THE LANDS WHICH HE FARMED HIMSELF

THEN there came the unexpected news of the death of the wife of Herlewin of Rungton. She held a charter by which she was to have that township for her life, and the abbot said, "Yesterday I would have given sixty marks to free that manor, now the Lord has freed it." Then when he had come and had received the township into his hand without any delay, and on the morrow had gone to Tilleney which was a part of that manor, there came to him a certain knight offering thirty marks that he might hold that carucate of land with what belonged to it on the same terms as before, namely, four pounds a year. This the abbot refused, and he took thence that year five and twenty pounds, and in the next year twenty pounds.

This and other similar events led him to keep all things in his hand; as it is written in another place, "Cæsar was everything." Nor was he slack, but caused first of all barns and cattlesheds to be built; he was anxious to cultivate the plough lands above all things; he was careful in maintaining the woods, and in giving and reducing these he made great profit for himself.

The one manor of Thorp alone he confirmed under his charter to a certain Englishman, a man adscript to the soil, in whose fidelity he had the fullest confidence, because he was a good farmer and because he knew no French.

HOW ABBOT SAMSON WAS MADE A JUSTICE, AND HOW HE BORE HIMSELF IN THIS OFFICE

SEVEN months had not yet passed since his election, and, behold! letters of the lord pope were sent to him appointing him a judge for hearing causes. In the performance of this work he was rude and inexperienced, though he was skilled in the liberal arts and in

A.D. 1182.
NOVEMBER.

the holy scriptures, as being a literate man, brought up in the schools and a ruler of scholars, and renowned and well proved in his own work. He therefore associated with himself two clerks who were learned in the law and joined them with him, using their advice in church matters, while he spent his leisure in studying the decrees and decretal letters. And the result was that in a little while he was regarded as a discreet judge, by reason of the books which he had read and the causes which he had tried, and as one who proceeded in the cases which he tried according to the form of law. And for this cause one said, "Cursed be the court of this abbot, where neither gold nor silver profit me to confound my enemy!"

In course of time, he became somewhat skilled in temporal matters, being guided by his commonsense, for his mind was so subtle that all men wondered, and Osbert FitzHerbert, the under-sheriff, used to say, "This abbot is given to disputation; if he goes on as he has begun, he will blind us all, however many we be." But the abbot, being approved in these matters, was made a justice in eyre, though he kept himself from error and wandering. But "envy seeks out the highest." His men complained to him in the court

of St. Edmund since he would not give judgment
hastily or believe every spirit, but proceeded in a judicial manner, knowing that the merits of the cases of
suitors are made clear by discussion.   It was said that
he would not do justice to any complainant, unless
money were given or promised ; and because his aspect
was acute and penetrating, and his face, like Cato's,
rarely smiling, it was said that his mind lent rather to
severity than to mercy.   Moreover. when he took
fines for any crime, it was said that judgment rejoiced
against mercy, for in the opinion of many, when it
came to a matter of taking money, he rarely remitted
that which he might lawfully take.

So his wisdom increased, as well as his care in
managing affairs, and in improving his state, and in
spending honourably.

HOW SOME MEN MADE COMPLAINT AGAINST THE ABBOT

But hereupon many of his adversaries raised objec
tions.   For they said that he received what he would
from the sacristy, and spared his own money, and
allowed his corn to lie in the barns until such time as
the price should be high.   They said that he managed

his manors in a way different from that of his predecessors; that he burdened his cellarer with guests who should rather have been received by the abbot, so that the abbot might win repute as a wise man and one who was clever and provident at the end of the year, but the monastery and its officials be thought ignorant and wasteful.

To these charges I used to answer that if he took anything from the sacristry, he employed it for the use of the church; and that no envious person could deny this. And to speak the truth, much more good and much greater good was done with the offerings of the sacristy during the fifteen years after his election than in the forty years preceding.

To the others who objected that the abbot went often to his manors, I was wont to answer and to excuse him by saying that the abbot was happier and in better spirits anywhere than at home. This also was the truth, whether on account of the constant complaints which came to him, or on account of those who told him rumours concerning himself. Accordingly, it often happened that his appearance was stern, and that so he lost much favour and grace with the guests, though he satisfied them with food and drink.

HOW THE AUTHOR TALKED WITH THE ABBOT CONCERNING THE SADNESS OF HIS MANNER

But I noticed this, and taking a favourable occasion, as I was with him alone, said, "There are two things in which you make me marvel greatly." And when he asked what they were, I said, "One is, that you, in the circumstances in which you are placed, favour the opinion of those of Melun who say that from a false premiss nothing can follow, and other foolish things." And when he answered what he would to this, I added, "The other thing at which I marvel is that you do not show a smiling face at home as you do elsewhere, nor remain among the brothers who cherish you, and love you, and have chosen you to be their lord, but are rarely with them, nor do you then rejoice with them, so they say."

When he heard this, his expression changed, and he answered, with bowed head, "You are a fool, and speak as a fool. You should know the saying of Solomon, Hast thou many daughters; show not thyself cheerful toward them." Then I was silent, and from that time placed a guard on my lips.

Yet on another occasion I said, "Lord, I heard you

this night keeping watch after matins and breathing heavily contrary to your wont." And he answered, " Is it not strange. You share my good things, food, and drink, and riding, and the like. But you think little of the toil of providing for the house and house-hold, of the many and arduous labours which are a pastor's care. These make me anxious, and cause me to groan and be troubled in spirit." Thereupon I raised my hands to heaven and answered, " From so great anxiety, almighty and merciful Lord, deliver me !"

I heard the abbot say that if he were in that condi-tion in which he had been before he became a monk, and had five or six marks income wherewith he might support himself in the schools, he would never become either monk or abbot. And on another occasion, he said with an oath that had he known beforehand what care there was in ruling an abbey, and how great that care was, he would far rather have been almoner or librarian, than abbot and lord. And he declared that he had ever longed for the post of librarian above all others. Yet who would believe such things? Not I; no, not I; but that as I lived with him day and night for six years, I know fully the merit of his life and the wisdom of his mind.

CONCERNING A DREAM WHICH THE ABBOT HAD WHEN A BOY

ONCE he told me how when he was a boy of nine years, he dreamed that he stood before the doors of the cemetery of St. Edmund, and that the devil wished to seize him with his outstretched arms. But the blessed Edmund, who stood near, received him into his arms; and when he had cried out in his sleep, "St. Edmund, help me!" though he had never heard the saint named before, he awoke. Then his mother was amazed at his loud cry and at his words. And when she had heard the dream, she took him to St. Edmund's, that he might pray there. So coming to the gate of the cemetery, he said, "Mother mine! see this place! See, the very door which I beheld in my dreams, when the devil would have taken me." And he knew the place, he said, as if he had already seen it with his carnal eye.

The abbot himself explained the dream, saying that the devil in it meant the joys of this world which would have enticed him; but that the blessed Edmund embraced him, since he would have him become a monk of his church.

HOW THE ABBOT RESTRAINED HIS TEMPER THAT HE MIGHT NOT OFFEND

ONCE when it was told him that certain of those in the monastery murmured on account of some act of his, he said to me, as I was near him, " God, God, it is most expedient that I should be mindful of that dream which was dreamed concerning me before I became abbot, to the effect that I should raven as a wolf. Of a truth, I fear this above all earthly things, that my house may do something which may make it lawful for me to raven. But so it is, that when they say or do aught against my will, I call to mind that dream, and though I raven in spirit, groaning and gnashing my teeth in secret, I put force on myself that I may raven neither in word nor in deed. And hidden grief chokes me, and my heart burns within me."

But though he was naturally choleric and easily moved to wrath, yet from respect for his office he generally restrained his anger, albeit with much grief of mind. Of this also he often spoke, saying "I have seen this and that, I have heard this and that, and yet have I borne it patiently."

HOW THE ABBOT FORBADE SECRET AC-CUSATIONS, AND HOW HE ORDERED THE RESTORATION OF ALL PRIVATE SEALS

ONCE as he sat in the chapter, the abbot spoke certain words whereby he seemed to court the favour of the monastery with success. " I will not," he said, " that any come to me to accuse other, unless he will declare the same openly. But if any desire to act otherwise, I will publicly announce the name of the accuser. And I will also that every monk shall have free access to me, that he may talk with me of his needs when he will." Now this he said because the chief men of our house in the days of abbot Hugh, wishing nothing to be done in the monastery save through them, decreed that no cloistered monk should speak with the abbot, unless he had first shown to the abbot's chaplain that which he desired to say to the abbot and the reason.

One day he commanded in the chapter that all who had seals of their own should restore them to him, and so it was done ; and thirty and three seals were found. He himself clearly declared the reason for this command, and forbade any official to contract any debt above the sum of twenty shillings without the consent of the prior and monastery, as had been wont to be done in the past. Then he restored the prior and sacristan their seals and retained the others.

CONCERNING FURTHER REGULATIONS WHICH THE ABBOT MADE

At another time he ordered that all the keys of the chests, cupboards, and hampers should be given up to him, and forbade anyone henceforth to have any chest or anything locked up, save by permission, or to possess anything of any description except such things as the rule allowed. However, he gave general permission to all of us to have money to the value of two shillings, if perchance this should be given to us in charity. The leave was still conditional on the money being expended for the benefit of poor relations or in pious uses.

On another occasion the abbot said that he wished to maintain our ancient custom in the matter of the reception of guests, so that when the abbot was at home he should receive all guests of whatever condition, except religious men, and except priests of secular habit, and except their men, who should come to the doors of the court by instruction of their masters. If, however, the abbot should not be at home, all guests of whatever condition should be received by the cellarer, up to the number of thirteen horses. But if a layman or clerk should come with more than thirteen horses, they should be received by the servants of the abbot, either within or without the court, at the expense of the abbot. All religious men, even bishops, if by chance they were monks, were to be the care of the cellarer and entertained at the expense of the monastery, unless the abbot were desirous of showing them honour and of receiving them in his hall at his own expense.

CONCERNING THE APPEARANCE AND PRIVATE CHARACTER OF THE ABBOT

Abbot Samson was below the average height, almost bald; his face was neither round nor oblong; his nose was prominent and his lips thick; his eyes were clear and his glance penetrating; his hearing was excellent; his eyebrows arched, and frequently shaved; and a little cold soon made him hoarse. On the day of his election he was forty-seven, and had been a monk for seventeen years. In his ruddy beard there were a few grey hairs, and still fewer in his black and curling hair. But in the course of the first fourteen years after his election all his hair became white as snow.

He was an exceedingly temperate man; he possessed great energy and a strong constitution, and was fond both of riding and walking, until old age prevailed upon him and moderated his ardour in these respects. When he heard the news of the capture of the cross and the fall of Jerusalem, he began to wear under garments made of horse-hair, and a horse-hair shirt, and gave up the use of flesh and meat. None the less, he willed that flesh should be placed before him as he sat at table, that the alms might be increased. He ate sweet milk, honey, and similar sweet things, far more readily than any other food.

He hated liars, drunkards, and talkative persons; for virtue ever loves itself and spurns that which is contrary to it. He blamed those who grumbled about their meat and drink, and especially monks who so grumbled, and personally kept to the same manners which he had observed when he was a cloistered monk. Moreover, he had this virtue in himself that he never desired to change the dish which was placed before him. When I was a novice, I wished to prove whether this was really true, and as I happened to serve in the refectory, I thought to place before him food which would have offended any other man, in a very dirty and broken dish. But when he saw this, he was as it were blind to it. Then, as there was some delay, I repented of what I had done, and straightway seized the dish, changed the food and dish for better, and carried it to him. He, however, was angry at the change, and disturbed.

He was an eloquent man, speaking both French and Latin, but rather careful of the good sense of that which he had to say than of the style of his words. He could read books written in English very well, and was wont to preach to the people in English, but in the dialect of Norfolk where he was born and bred. It was for this reason that he ordered a pulpit to be placed in the church, for the sake of those who heard him and for purposes of ornament.

The abbot further appeared to prefer the active to the contemplative life, and praised good officials more than good monks. He rarely commended anyone solely on account of his knowledge of letters, unless the man happened to have knowledge of secular affairs, and if he chanced to hear of any prelate who had given up his pastoral work and become a hermit, he did not praise him for this. He would not praise men who were too kindly, saying, "He who strives to please all men, deserves to please none."

HOW ABBOT SAMSON DEALT WITH FLATTERERS

Now in the first year of his abbacy he seemed to hate all flatterers, and especially those who were monks. But in course of time he appeared to listen to them with some willingness, and to treat them more graciously. Once a certain one of our brothers, who was skilled in this art, had bent his knees before him, and under pretence of giving him counsel, had poured the oil of flattery into his ears, while I stood at a distance and smiled. Then when the brother had gone, the abbot called me and asked me why I had been smiling, and I answered that the world was full of flatterers.

And the abbot said, " My son, I have been flattered for a long while, and therefore I cannot attend to flattery. There must be much pretence and much concealment that the peace of the monastery may be preserved. I will hear them speak, but they will not deceive me, if I can prevent it, as they deceived my predecessor, who gave such unconsidered attention to

them that for a long while before his death he had
nothing wherewith to feed himself or his household,
save that which he borrowed from creditors.   And on
the day of his burial there was nothing which could
be distributed among the poor, save fifty shillings
which were received from Richard the tenant of
Palgrave, because on the same day he entered on the
tenancy of Palgrave; and this money the same Richard
afterwards paid again to the officials of the king, who
exacted the full rent for the royal use."   And with
these words I was reassured.

HOW ABBOT SAMSON MANAGED HIS HOUSEHOLD

He laboured to secure a well-regulated house, and
a household large, but not larger than was right, and
he took care that the weekly allowance which in the
time of his predecessor had not been enough for five
days, should last him for eight days, or nine, or ten,
if he were on his manors and there were no great
coming of guests.   Every week, moreover, he audited
the expenses of his house, not through an agent, but
in person, a thing which his predecessor had never
been accustomed to do.

For his first seven years he had four dishes in his house, afterwards only three, if one excludes presents, and game from his parks and fish from his ponds. And if he happened to keep anyone for a while in his house at the request of some great man or of one of his friends, or messengers, or minstrels, or any such person, he used to take any opportunity of crossing the sea or going a long journey, and so prudently freed himself from so great expense.

HOW THE ABBOT TREATED THOSE MONKS WITH WHOM HE HAD BEEN INTIMATE BEFORE HE BECAME ABBOT

THOSE monks whom the abbot, before he acquired the abbacy, had treated as his most cherished and intimate friends, he seldom raised to official positions on the score of his former intimacy with them, unless they were fit persons. Therefore some of our number, who had favoured his election as abbot, said that he showed them less favour than was their due, who had loved him before he was abbot, and that those rather were cherished by him who had slandered him both openly and secretly, and in the hearing of many had publicly declared him to be a hot-tempered man, one who was unsociable, conceited, and a Norfolk cheat. But, just as after he received the abbacy he made no injudicious exhibition of affection or of a desire to honour his former friends, so also he did not show towards the others any of that rancour or hatred which they deserved, returning good for evil on many occasions, and doing good to those who persecuted him.

He had also a characteristic which I have never seen in any other man, namely, that he had a strong affection for many to whom he never or seldom showed a loving face, which the common saying declares to be usual, when it says, "Where love is, there the glance follows." And there was another noteworthy thing, that he wittingly suffered loss from his servants in temporal matters, and allowed that he suffered it; but, as I believe, the reason for this was that he waited for a fit season when the matter might be conveniently remedied, or that by concealing his knowledge he might avoid greater loss.

HOW THE ABBOT TREATED HIS RELATIONS

FOR his relations he displayed moderate affection, but yet no less tender than that which others are wont to show, since he had no relatives within the third degree, or pretended that he had not. I have, however, heard him assert that he had relations who were noble and distinguished, but that he would never at any time recognise them as relations. For, as he said, they would be rather a burden than a source of advantage to him if they knew of their relationship. On the other hand, he wished to have as kin those who had claimed kinship with him when he was a poor cloistered monk.

Some of his relations, in cases where he thought them useful and capable men, he appointed to various offices in his house, and others he entrusted with the wardenship of manors. But any whom he proved to be unfaithful he drove far from him, without hope of return.

He held as his dear kinsman a certain man of low birth, who had managed his inheritance faithfully and served him devotedly in his boyhood. To this man's son, who was a clerk, he gave the first church which fell vacant after his accession to the abbacy, and he also promoted all the man's other sons.

HOW THE ABBOT WAS MINDFUL OF THOSE WHO HAD SHOWN KINDNESS TO HIM IN THE PAST, AND HOW HE TREATED THOSE WHO HAD BEEN HARSH

THERE was a certain chaplain who had maintained him in the schools of Paris by the sale of holy water, when he was poor. This man the abbot caused to be summoned to him, and conferred on him an ecclesiastical benefice, with the position of vicar, whereby he might be supported.

He granted to a certain servant of his predecessor food and clothing for all the days of his life, this man being he who had placed fetters on him at the command of his lord when he was imprisoned.

When FitzElias, the cup-bearer of abbot Hugh, came to do him homage for his father's land, the abbot said to him in open court, "I have delayed now for seven years to receive your homage for the land which abbot Hugh gave to your father, since that gift was to the detriment of the manor of

Elmswell. Now I give way, since I am mindful of the good which your father did to me when I was in bonds. For he sent to me some of the very wine which his lord drank, with a message that I should be of good courage in God."

When master William, son of master William of Diss, asked of his grace for the vicarage of the church of Chevington, he answered, "Your father was master of the schools, and when I was a poor clerk he allowed me to enter the school without terms and of his grace, and to have the opportunity of learning. And I, for the sake of God, grant you that which you ask."

Two knights also from Risby, William and Norman, were by chance judged to be at his mercy, and he thus addressed them in the presence of all: "When I was a cloistered monk, I was sent to Durham on the business of our church. And as I was returning thence by way of Risby, I was overtaken by a dark night, and sought entertainment from the lord Norman, but suffered an absolute denial. Then I went to the house of lord William and prayed for lodging, and was honourably received by him. For this cause I will take twenty shillings, the full penalty, without pity, from Norman; but I give thanks to

William, and gladly remit the due penalty of twenty shillings."

CONCERNING OTHER GOOD ACTS OF ABBOT SAMSON

A CERTAIN young girl, who was begging her bread from door to door, made complaint to the abbot that one of the sons of Richard FitzDrogo had assaulted her. This wrong, by the abbot's intervention, was at last settled for the sake of peace by the acceptance of one mark by the girl. The abbot further took four marks from the said Richard for leave to compound for his offence. But all these five marks he ordered to be given at once to a certain pedlar, on condition that he should marry the poor girl.

In the town of St. Edmund's the abbot bought stone houses, and appointed them for the maintenance of the schools. His reason for so doing was that thus the poor clerks might there be for ever free from paying rent for houses. Hitherto, for the payment of the rent, all the scholars, poor and rich alike, had been compelled to contribute a penny or a halfpenny twice a year.

BEFORE A.D. 1198.

HOW THE JEWS WERE DRIVEN FROM SAINT EDMUND'S

THE recovery of the manor of Mildenhall for one thousand one hundred silver marks, and the expulsion of the Jews from the town of St. Edmund's, and the foundation of a new hospital at Babewell, were signs of great value.

The lord abbot sought letters from the king that the Jews might be expelled from the town of St. Edmund's asserting that whatever is in the town of the blessed Edmund, or within the district subject to the jurisdiction of the monastery, belongs of right to the Saint, and that consequently the Jews ought either to be the men of St. Edmund, or else be driven from the town. Leave, therefore, was given to him to eject them, provided that they should have all their chattels, as well as the value of their houses and lands. And when they were sent forth, and under armed force were conducted to various towns, the abbot ordered that in every church and before every altar those should be solemnly excommunicated who should henceforth receive Jews or entertain them as guests in the town of St. Edmund's. This provision was afterwards modified by the justices of the king,

A.D. 1190.

to the effect that if Jews should come to the great pleas of the abbot in order to exact debts due to them from their debtors, then for this reason they might be entertained for two days and two nights in the town, and depart in peace on the third day.

HOW THE ABBOT SECURED THE MANOR OF MILDENHALL, AND ENDOWED THE HOSPITAL AT BABWELL

THE abbot offered king Richard five hundred marks for the manor of Mildenhall, saying that the annual value of that manor was seventy pounds, and that it had been enrolled for that amount in the great roll of Winchester.

A.D. 1189.
SEPTEMBER.

And when he thought that he would obtain his desire in this matter, the settlement of the affair was postponed to the following day. In the interval there came one to the king and told him that the manor was worth quite one hundred pounds. And so when the abbot urged his request on the morrow, the king said to him, " My lord abbot, it is useless for you to make this petition to me. Either you shall give me a thousand marks, or you shall not have the manor."

But queen Eleanor, who according to the custom of the realm, had the right to receive a hundred marks when the king received a thousand, took from us a great gold chalice of the value of a hundred marks, and restored this same chalice to us for the good of the soul of king Henry her lord, who had originally given it to St. Edmund.

At a latter date, when the treasure of our church was carried to London for the ransom of king Richard, the queen redeemed the same chalice for a hundred marks and restored it to us, and received from us a charter in proof of our promise, made on the word of truth, that we would never for any reason alienate that chalice from our church.

A.D.
1193.

Now when this large sum of money had been collected with great difficulty and had been paid, the abbot, sitting in the chapter, said that he ought to share somewhat in so great an acquisition as that of so fair a manor. And the monastery answered, " That is just. Let it be done according to your will." And the abbot said that he might lawfully claim half of it, and showed that he had spent more than four hundred marks with great labour, but that he would be content with one portion of that manor, a place called Icklingham, and this was most readily granted to him by the monastery. Hearing this, the abbot said, " And I receive that portion of the land for my own purposes, not that I may keep it in my hand or to give to my relations, but that for the good of my soul and of the souls of all of you, I give it to the new hospital at Babwell, for the support of the poor and for the use of the hospital." So he spoke, and so it was done, and the act was afterwards confirmed by a charter from the king.

A.D.
1198.

These and other like things did abbot Samson, which are worthy to be written down and to be praised for all time. Yet he declared that he would have done nothing, unless in his time he could bring to pass that our church should be dedicated ; and when that had been accomplished, he asserted that he was ready to die. Moreover, he said that for the doing of this thing he would expend two thousand marks of silver, if so the king might be present and the affair carried through with due ceremony.

CONCERNING THE CHURCH OF WOOL-PIT, AND HOW IT WAS SECURED FOR THE ABBEY

THE abbot learnt that the church of Woolpit was vacant, for Walter of Coutances had been elected to

the bishopric of Lincoln. And presently he summoned together the prior
and most of the monastery, and taking
up his tale, said : " You know well what great labours
I have undergone in the matter of the church of
Woolpit, and how to secure it for your exclusive use
I journeyed to Rome by your advice,
in the days of the schism between
Alexander and Octavian. And I
traversed Italy at the time when all
clerks bearing letters of pope Alexander were seized,
some of them being imprisoned and others hanged,
and others, after having their noses and lips cut off,
were sent back to the pope to his shame and confusion. I, however, pretended that I was a Scot, and
put on Scottish dress, and adopted the manners of a
Scot. And I often shook my staff as they shake the
weapon which they call a gaveloc at those who mocked
me, shouting threatening words in the manner of the
Scots. To those who met me and asked me who
I was, I answered nothing except " Ride, ride Rome,
turne Cantwereberei." I acted thus that so I might
conceal my purpose, and as a Scot might safely reach
Rome. Then when I had obtained from the lord
pope such letters as I desired, on my homeward way

In left margin:

A.D.
1183.

Between
A.D. 1159 and
A.D. 1162

I passed by a certain castle as the road led me from the city. And, lo! the officers of the castle surrounded me, laying hold on me, and crying, "This wanderer, who makes himself out to be a Scot, is either a spy or one bearing letters of the false pope Alexander." And while they closely examined my clothes and boots and undergarments, and even the old shoes, which I carried on my shoulders in the Scottish manner, I put my hand into the little bag which I carried, and in which the letter of the lord pope was contained, lying under a little cup from which I was wont to drink. And the Lord God and St. Edmund willing it, I drew out the writing and the cup together, so that, stretching my hand on high, I held the writ underneath the cup. And they saw the cup, is it true, but they did not notice the writ. And so I escaped their hands, in the name of the Lord. Whatever money I had on me they took away, so that it was necessary for me to beg for my bread, spending nothing, until I came to England. But when I heard that the church was given to Geoffrey Ridel, my soul was grieved with the thought that my labour had been vain. So when I reached home I secretly cast myself before the shrine of St. Edmund, for I feared that the lord abbot would

seize me and cast me into prison, who had deserved
no ill. And there was no monk who dared to speak
with me, and no layman who dared supply me with
food, save secretly. At length, the abbot took counsel
and exiled me to Acre, and there I long remained.
These and many other countless ills I have suffered
for the sake of the church of Woolpit. But blessed
be God, Who maketh all things work together for
good! Behold! the church for which I have borne
so many hardships, is given into my hand, and now
I have the power to give it to whomsoever I will,
since it is vacant. And I restore it to the monastery,
and for its sole use I assign the ancient customary
due or pension of ten marks, which you have lost for
more than sixty years. I would give it in its entirety
to you with pleasure were I able to do so; but I
know that the bishop of Norwich would forbid this,
or if he were to grant it, he would make it an excuse
to demand subjection and obedience from you, which
is neither wise nor convenient. Therefore let us do
what we may lawfully do. Let us place there a
clerk as vicar to answer to the bishop for the spiritu-
alities, and to you for the ten marks; and I wish, if
you agree, that the vicarage may be given to some
relative of Roger de Hengham, a monk and your

brother, who was my companion in that journey to
Rome, and was exposed to the same dangers as I was
and for the same cause."

At these words we all arose and gave thanks; and
Hugh, a clerk and a brother of the said Roger, was
received in the said church, saving our annual pension
of ten marks.

HOW THE ABBOT DISPUTED WITH THE ARCHBISHOP CONCERNING THE MANOR OF ELEIGH

In a manor of the monks of Canterbury, which is
called Eleigh, and which is in the hundred of the
abbot, there chanced to be a murder.
But the archbishop's men would not
allow the murderers to take their trial
in the court of St. Edmund. Then the abbot made
complaint to king Henry, and said that archbishop
Baldwin was claiming the liberties of our church for
himself on the ground of a new charter which the
king had given to the church of Canterbury after the
death of the blessed Thomas.

Then the king answered that he had never given a
charter to the prejudice of our church, and that he

CIRCA
A.D. 1186.

did not wish to take from the blessed Edmund anything which he had formerly possessed. On hearing this, the abbot said to his intimate advisers: "It is wiser counsel that the archbishop should make complaint of me than that I should make complaint of the archbishop. I wish to place myself in possession of this liberty, and then I will defend myself with the help of St. Edmund, in whose right our charters bear witness that this liberty is."

Accordingly, unexpectedly, and very early in the morning, with the help of Robert de Cokefield, about eighty armed men were sent to the town of Eleigh, and took those three murderers by surprise and brought them bound to St. Edmund's, and cast them into the dungeon of the prison. And when the archbishop made complaint of this, Ranulf Glanvill, the justiciar, commanded that those men should be bound by surety and pledges to stand their trial in the court wherein they ought to stand it; and the abbot was summoned to come to the court of the king and to make reply concerning the violence and injury which he was said to have done to the archbishop. And the abbot many times presented himself at the court, without attempting to make excuse.

At last, at the beginning of the fasting time, they

stood before the king in the chapter-house of Canterbury, and the chapters of the two
churches were read publicly. And
the lord king answered, "These
charters are of equal age, and come from the same
king Edward. I know not what to say, save that the
charters are contradictory." To this the abbot replied, "Whatever may be said about the charters, we
are seised of the liberty, and have been in the past,
and on this point I will submit to the verdict of the two
counties, Norfolk and Suffolk, which will allow this."

A.D. 1187.
11TH. FEBRUARY.

Archbishop Baldwin, however, having first taken
counsel with his men, said that the men of Norfolk
and Suffolk loved St. Edmund greatly, and that a large
part of those counties was under the rule of the abbot,
and therefore he would not abide by their arbitration.
But the king was angry and offended at that, and rising
up, left the place, saying, "He that is able to receive
it, let him receive it." And thus the matter was
postponed, and is still undecided.

But I saw that some of the men of the monks of
Canterbury were wounded to the death by the rustics
of the township of Midling, which is situated in the
hundred of St. Edmund, and as they knew that the
prosecutor is bound to go to the court of the defen-

dant, they preferred to be silent and to hide the matter, rather than complain of it to the abbot or his officers, since they were in nowise willing to come and plead in the court of St. Edmund.

After these things the men of Eleigh set up a certain measure for the doing of justice in cases where bread and corn had been measured with false measures, and the abbot made complaint of this to the lord bishop of Ely, who was at that time justiciar and chancellor. But he would not hear the abbot, because he was alleged to be scenting the archbishopric, which was then vacant. When, however, he had come among us, and was received as a legate, before he departed, he made prayer at the shrine of the holy martyr. And the abbot, seizing the opportunity, said in the hearing of all who were present, "My lord bishop, the liberty, which the monks of Canterbury claim, is the right of St. Edmund, whose body is here, and as you will not assist me to protect the liberty of his church, I put a complaint between you and him. Henceforth he may secure his right." The chancellor did not condescend to make any answer, and within a year was forced to leave England, and suffered divine vengeance.

A.D. 1191.

A.D. 1191.
29TH OCTOBER.

But when the same chancellor had returned from Germany and had landed at Ipswich, and spent the night at Hitcham, a report came to the abbot that the chancellor wished to pass through St. Edmund's, and to hear mass with us on the morrow.   Therefore the abbot forbade the celebration of the divine offices while the chancellor was present in the church, for he said that he had heard in London that the bishop of London had pronounced the chancellor excommunicate, in the presence of six bishops, especially for the violence which he had done to the archbishop of York, at Dover, and that the said chancellor, while excommunicate, had departed from England.

A.D.
1193.

A.D. 1191.
SEPTEMBER.

Accordingly, when the chancellor came among us on the morrow, he found no one to chant mass for him, either clerk or monk.   But the priest, indeed, who stood at the first mass and at the canon of the mass, and the other priests by the altars, ceased, and stood with unmoved lips, until a messenger came and said that he had left the church.   The chancellor took no notice openly, but he did many ills to the abbot, until, by the mediation of friends, they both returned to the kiss of peace.

HOW THE ABBOT WISHED TO TAKE THE CROSS, AND HOW HE OFFERED TO SEEK KING RICHARD IN GERMANY

WHEN king Henry had taken the cross and was come less than a month later that he might pray among us, the abbot secretly made for himself a cross of linen cloth. Then, holding in one hand the cross and a needle and thread, he sought leave from the king that he might take the cross. But leave was refused him, for John, bishop of Norwich, opposed it, and said that it was not well for the land, nor safe for the counties of Norfolk and Suffolk, that the bishop of Norwich and the abbot of St. Edmund's should go away at the same time.

A.D. 1188.
21ST JANUARY.

When news had reached London of the capture of king Richard, and of his imprisonment in Germany, and the barons had met to take counsel on the matter, the abbot stood forth in their presence, and said that he was ready to seek his lord the king. He said that he would search for him in diguise or in any other way, until he found him and had certain knowledge of him. And from this speech he gained great praise for himself.

A.D. 1193.

HOW THE ABBOT RESISTED THE AU-
THORITY OF THE LEGATE

When the chancellor, the bishop of Ely, filled the office of legate and held a council at London, he pro-posed certain decrees against the black monks, talking of their wandering to the shrines of St. Thomas and of St. Edmund under pretence of pilgrimage, and speaking against the abbots, mentioning a certain number of horses which they ought to have. Then abbot Samson answered, "We will not receive any decree which is contrary to the rule of St. Benedict, which allows the abbots a free hand in the control of their monks. And I serve the barony of St. Edmund and his realm ; thirteen horses are not enough for me, as they may be for some other abbots, unless I have addi-tional horses for the administration of the justice of the king."

A.D.
1190.

OF THE CONDUCT OF THE ABBOT WHILE
KING RICHARD WAS IN CAPTIVITY

After the capture of king Richard, there was war throughout England. And the abbot with the whole

A.D.
1193.

monastery solemnly excommunicated all who stirred up war and broke the peace, showing no fear of earl John, the king's brother, or of any other, whence he was called a great-souled abbot. And after doing this, he went to the siege of Windsor, where he appeared in arms with some other abbots of England, and had his own standard. He had there also with him many knights at great expense, and he gained a reputation rather for skill in the council than for virtue.

But we who were cloistered monks considered this course of action to be fraught with danger, fearing lest some future abbot might be compelled to go to war in person. Then, when a truce had been granted, he went to Germany, and there sought the king with many gifts.

CONCERNING THAT WHICH BEFEL CERTAIN KNIGHTS WHO DESIRED TO HOLD A TOURNAMENT CONTRARY TO THE WISH OF THE ABBOT

AFTER the return of king Richard to England, leave was granted to knights to hold tournaments,

A.D.
1193.

and many gathered between Thetford and St. Edmund's for this purpose. Then the abbot forbade them, but they resisted him, and did all that they desired.

On another occasion twenty-four young men, sons of nobles, came fully armed with their followers to have their revenge at the same place. And when they had made an end, they returned to the town to lodge there. But when the abbot heard of it, he commanded the gates to be closed and all of them to be shut within the town. The following day was the vigil 28TH JUNE of the apostles Peter and Paul. Therefore, when they had given their word that they would not leave the town without permission, they all ate with the abbot on that day. After the meal, when the abbot had retired to his private chamber, they all arose and began to laugh and sing. And sending to the town for wine, they drank and afterwards shouted loudly, and so they kept the abbot and the monastery from their sleep, and did everything to mock the abbot. So they spent the day until the evening, nor would they cease at the abbot's command.

Finally, when evening was come, they broke the bars of the gates of the city, and forced their way out. The abbot solemnly excommunicated them all, by the advice of archbishop Hubert, who was then justiciar, and many of them made reparation and sought absolution.

CONCERNING THE MISSIONS OF THE ABBOT TO THE PAPAL COURT

THE abbot sent many messengers to Rome, and not in vain. The first whom he sent, immediately after his benediction, obtained in detail all the liberties and rights which had been granted to his predecessors, even in the days of schism. Afterwards he obtained that he might give episcopal benediction wherever he might be, and he was the first of the abbots of England to gain this. This right he won for himself and for his successors.

A.D. 1182.
31ST MARCH.

A.D. 1187.
21ST JANUARY.

A.D. 1188.

At a later date he acquired complete exemption for himself and for his successors from all the archbishops of Canterbury, a privilege which abbot Hugh had secured for himself alone. In these confirmations of privileges abbot Samson caused the inclusion of many new liberties, to the great freedom and safety of our church.

Then a certain clerk came to the abbot, bearing letters asking for the grant of some ecclesiastical benefice. And the abbot drew from his desk seven apostolic letters, with leaden seals hanging to them, and answered as follows: "See the apostolic letters, whereby different popes seek that ecclesiastical benefices may be given to this or that clerk. When then I have satisfied those who come first I will give you a benefice, since he who first comes to the mill ought to grind first."

HOW THE ABBOT MET THE CLAIM OF EARL DE CLARE TO BEAR THE STANDARD OF SAINT EDMUND

A GENERAL summons was issued in the hundred of Risbridge that the complaint and trial of earl de Clare might be heard at Witham. And he was accompanied by a great crowd of barons and knights, while Earl Alberic and many others were present, and he said that his officers had given him to understand that they were wont to receive five shillings for his use from the hundred and from the officers of the hundred, which were now wrongfully withheld. He also alleged that his predecessors had been enfeoffed with the land of Alfric, son of Withgar, who was formerly lord of that hundred, at the time of the conquest of England.

But the abbot, considering in his own mind and not stirring from his place, answered, "My lord earl,

your words astonish me! Your case is not proven.
King Edward gave to St. Edmund, and confirmed
the gift in his charter, this whole hundred, and no
mention was made of these five shillings. Do you
tell us for what service, or on what grounds, you
claim those five shillings!" And the earl, having
consulted his men, replied that he had the right to
bear the standard of St. Edmund in the host, and
for this reason those five shillings were due to him.
Then the abbot answered, "In truth, it seems an unworthy thing that so great a man as the earl de Clare
should receive so small a gift for so important a service,
but it is small harm to the abbot of St. Edmund's to
give five shillings. Earl Roger Bigod holds that he is
seised of the land, and declares that he is seised of
the duty of bearing the standard of St. Edmund,
and he bore it when the earl of Leicester was taken
and the Flemings destroyed. Moreover, Thomas de
Mendham says that this right belongs to him.
But when you shall have proved against them that
this right is yours, I will willingly pay the five shillings
which you demand." Then the earl answered that
he would speak of the matter to earl Roger his
relative, and so the matter has not been decided to
this day.

CONCERNING THE CASE OF ADAM DE COKEFIELD

Now, when Robert de Cokefield was dead, his son Adam came with his relatives, earl Roger Bigod, and
many other powerful men. And they

A.D.
1191.

sought from the abbot the holdings of the said Adam, and especially for half the hundred of Cosford, to be held at an annual rent of a hundred shillings, as if this was his by hereditary right, and declared that his father and grandfather had held it for eighty years past and more.

But the abbot, when he had opportunity for speaking, put his two fingers in his two eyes, and said, "May I lose these eyes in that day and hour in the which I grant a hundred to any man to hold by hereditary right, unless the king, who is able both to take away the abbacy from me and to deprive me of life, force me to do this thing." And he gave the reason for this saying, and added, "If any man hold a hundred by hereditary right, and if he commit an offence of any sort against the king for the which he ought to be disinherited, forthwith the sheriff of Suffolk and the officers of the king would seize the hundred, and would exercise authority within our borders. And if they should have the wardenship of this hundred, then would the liberty of eight hundreds and a half be imperilled."

Then he addressed himself to Adam, and said "If you, who claim hereditary right in this hundred, were to marry any free woman, who held even a single acre of land from the king in chief, the king after your death would have seisin of the whole of your land and the wardship of your son, if he were a minor, and thus the officers of the king would enter the hundred of St. Edmund to the prejudice of the abbot. For the matter of that, your father made acknowledgment to me that he claimed no hereditary right in that hundred, and because his service pleased me, I permitted him to hold it all the days of his life, as his deserts warranted."

After he had thus spoken, much money was offered to the abbot, but he could not be turned from his purpose either by prayer or present. At the last it was thus agreed between them : Adam abandoned the right which he had verbally claimed in the hundred, and the abbot confirmed to him all his other lands. No mention was made, however, of our township of Cokefield, and it is believed that he had no charter concerning it. Semere and Groton he was to hold for the term of his life.

HOW THE MILL WHICH HERBERT THE DEAN HAD BUILT WAS OVERTURNED

HERBERT the dean built a windmill on Haberdon. When the abbot heard this, he was so wroth that he would hardly eat, or speak a single word. On the morrow, after he had heard mass, he commanded the sacristan that without delay he should cause his carpenter to go thithers and overturn everything, and place the wood with which it had been built in safe keeping.

And the dean heard this, and he came, saying that he was by law able to do this on his freehold land, and that the profit which may come from the wind ought to be denied to no man. He said also that he intended to grind his own corn there and not that of other men, that he might not be thought to have done this thing to the detriment of neighbouring mills.

And the abbot, still angry, replied, "I thank you as much as if you had cut off both my feet; by the face of God, I will never eat bread until that building be overturned. You are an old man, and you ought to know that neither the king nor his justiciar may change anything or build anything within the jurisdiction of the monastery, without the leave of the abbot and the house. And who are you, that you are so very presumptuous? Nor is this without harm to my mills, as you pretend, for the burghers go to your mill, and grind their corn at their pleasure, while I cannot lawfully hinder them, since they are free men. And I would not allow even the mill of the cellarer, which has been newly built, to stand, had it not been that it was built before I was abbot. Depart," he went on, "depart. Before you come to your house, you will hear what has come to pass in the matter of your mill."

Then the dean, fearing before the face of the abbot, took counsel with his son, master Stephen, and anticipated the servants of the sacristan, and caused the mill which had been built by his own servants to be destroyed without delay. And so it was, that when the men of the sacristan came there, they found nothing to overthrow.

HOW THE RIGHT OF THE ABBOT TO PRESENT TO CERTAIN CHURCHES WAS DISPUTED, AND WHAT BEFEL IN THE MATTER

THE right of the abbot to present to certain churches was disputed, and he gained the point. He also retained the right to present in certain other cases where that right had been disputed, in the cases of the churches of Westley, Meringthorpe, Bretenham, Weneling, Pakenham, Newton, and Bradfield in Norfolk, half the church of Boxford, the church of Scaldwell and the church of Endgate. All these he retained against the claim of others, and he recovered the right of presentation to three parts of the church of Dickleburgh. And in those portions he restored the holdings to the freehold of the church, saving the service due thence to the manor of Titshall.

But when the church of Boxford fell vacant, and an inquest was ordered in the matter, five knights came, tempting the abbot, and asking him what they should swear in that matter. But the abbot would not either give or promise them anything, and said, "When the time comes to make oath, say that which is right according to your conscience." Then they went away in anger, and by their oath, in an
inquest of darrein presentment, deprived him of the right of presenting to that church. This right he afterwards regained at great expense and by a payment of ten marks.

The abbot retained the church of Honington,

which had not been vacant, but to which his claim had been disputed in the time of Daniel de Hostelli, though he produced in evidence of his right a charter of William, bishop of Norwich, wherein it was provided that Robert de Valoniis, his father-in-law, had given that church to Ernald Lovell.

When half the church of Hopeton was vacant, a dispute arose on this matter between the abbot and

BEFORE
A.D. 1191.

Robert de Ulmo. And when a day for settling the matter was appointed at Hopeton, after much disputing, the abbot said to the same Robert, being moved thereto by some sudden impulse, "Swear in your own person that this right is yours, and I will grant that it is." And when the knight refused to swear, the matter was transferred with the assent of both parties to sixteen legal men of the hundred, who made oath that the right belonged to the abbot. Gilbert Fitz Ralph and Robert de Cokefield, the lords of that fief, were present, and gave their assent.

HOW ABBOT SAMSON DISPUTED WITH JORDAN DE ROS

THEN master Jordan de Ros, who had charter both from abbot Hugh and the said Robert, came forward, and addressing both parties, said that whichever of them proved his claim to the church, he ought to have the position of rector. He declared that he was rector of the whole church, and that the recently deceased clerk was his vicar, paying to him an annual income from that half, and in evidence he produced a charter of Walchelin the archdeacon.

Then the abbot was perturbed and angered with him, nor did he ever receive him into his favour until the same Jordan in the chapter of the monks of Thetford, owing to the abbot's insistence, resigned into the hands of the bishop, who was present there, that half absolutely, without any conditions or hope of recovery, in the presence of a number of clerks. When this had been done, the abbot said, "My lord bishop, I am bound on a promise to give the revenue to one of your clerks, and I will give the half of this church to whichsoever of your clerks you will." And the bishop asked that he would restore it in a friendly manner to the same Jordan, and thus Jordan received it by presentation from the abbot.

After this a dispute arose between the abbot and this same Jordan about the land of Herard in Harlow, as to whether or no it was a free fief of the church.

And when an inquest of twelve knights was ordered
on this matter, to be made in the king's court, by
leave of the justiciar Ranulf Glanvill it was made in
the court of the abbot at Harlow.   And the jurors
swore that they had never known that land divided
from the church, but yet that this land owed to the
abbot the same service as the land of Eustace and
certain other land of laymen in the same township
owed to him.

At last an agreement was reached between them on
the following terms : master Jordan in full court
acknowledged that this land was a lay fief, and that
he had no rights in it except by the grace of the
abbot.   And he was to hold that land all the days
of his life, paying an annual rent to the abbot for it
of twelve pence in commutation of all services.

HOW THE AUTHOR MADE A LIST OF THE ABBOT'S CHURCHES AS A GIFT TO THE ABBOT, AND THE NAMES OF THOSE CHURCHES

Now when, in the manner of the English, many
men gave many presents to the abbot, as to their

lord, on the day of the Circumcision of the Lord.
I, Jocelin, thought what I could give to him. And
I began to write out a list of all the churches which
are in the gift of the abbot, both on our manors and
on his, and the right values of the same, according as
they might be placed at firm at a time when the
price of corn was moderate. And when the beginning
of the next year came, I gave to the abbot that
schedule as my gift to him, and he received it with
great pleasure.

Then I, because I was then pleasing in his sight,
"thought in my heart" that I might say to him
that he should give some church to the monastery
and should assign it to the maintenance of hospitality.
as he had himself desired when he was a poor
cloistered monk, and as before his election he had
wished the brothers to swear, that he on whom the
lot of the abbacy should fall should do this. But
while I so thought I suddenly called to mind that
some other had already said to him this word, and
that I had heard the abbot answer that he could not
dismember his barony, that is, that he ought not to
reduce the liberty and dignity which abbot Hugh
and others, his predecessors, had possessed in the
matter of giving churches, which brought little or no

gain to the monastery. And for this cause I was silent.

Now the writing was as follows :—

"These are the churches on the manors and socages of the abbot : The church of Melford, valued at forty pounds ; Chevington, ten marks ; Saxham, twelve marks ; Hargrave, five marks ; Bretenham five marks ; Boxford, a hundred shillings ; the greater Fornham, a hundred shillings ; Stowe, a hundred shillings ; Honington, five marks ; Elmswell, three marks ; Cotton, twelve marks ; Brocford, five marks ; Palgrave, ten marks ; the greater Horningsherth, five marks ; Kingston, four marks ; Harlow, nineteen marks ; Stapleford, three marks ; Tivetshall, a hundred shillings ; Worlingworth and Bedingfield, twenty marks ; Saham, six marks ; half the church of Wortham, a hundred shillings ; Rungton, twenty marks ; Thorp, six marks ; Woolpit, with the pension excluded, a hundred shillings ; Rushbrook, five marks ; half the church of Hopeton, sixty shillings ; Riching-hall, six marks ; three parts of the church of Dickle-burgh, at the rate of over thirty shillings for each part ; half the church of Gislingham, four marks ; Icklingham, six marks ; the church of Mildenhall, which is worth forty marks, and half the church of

Wederden, some unknown quantity; Weneling, a hundred shillings; the church of Len, ten marks; that of Scaldwell, five marks; Warkton . . .

"These are the churches on the manors of the monastery:—Mildenhall, Barton, and Horningsherth, valued at twenty-five marks, exclusive of the pension; Rougham, fifteen marks, exclusive of the pension; Bradfield, five marks; Pakenham, thirty marks; South-rey, a hundred shillings; Risby, twenty marks; New-ton, four marks; Whepstead, fourteen marks; Fornham St. Genevieve, fifteen marks; Herningswell, nine marks; Fornham St. Martin, three marks; Ingham, ten marks; Lackford, a hundred shillings; Alpheton, ten marks; Cokefield, twenty marks; Semere, twelve marks; Groton, five marks; half the church of Fresing-feld, fourteen marks; Beccles. twenty marks; Broc, fifteen marks; Heldcercle, ten marks; Warkton, ten marks; Scaldwell, five marks; Westley, five marks; a church in Norwich, two marks, excluding the pension of herrings; and two churches in Colchester, three marks, excluding the pension of four shillings; Chels-worth, a hundred shillings; Meringthorp, four marks; half the church of Bradfield in Norfolk, three marks; staffacres, and foracres, and a third of the tithes of the demesnes of Wrabnesse, six marks."

HOW THE ABBOT FREED HIS CHURCH FROM CONTRIBUTION TO THE FINE INFLICTED ON NORFOLK AND SUFFOLK

THE two counties of Norfolk and Suffolk were adjudged by the itinerant justices to be fined at the king's

A.D
1187.

discretion for some fault, and fifty marks were imposed upon Norfolk and thirty upon Suffolk. And when some portion of that common fine was placed upon the lands of St. Edmund and sternly exacted, the abbot without delay went to the lord king, and we found him at Clarendon. And when a charter of king Edward, which freed the lands of St Edmund from all gelds and scot, had been shown to him, the king ordered by his letters that six knights of the county of Norfolk and six of that of Suffolk should be summoned to make inquest in the presence of the barons of the exchequer, as to whether the demesnes of St. Edmund ought to be quit of that general fine.

Then six knights were chosen, that so trouble and expense might be saved, and these because they held lands in both counties, namely, Hubert de Brisewood, W. FitzHervey, and William de Francheville, and three others. They went with us to London, and on behalf of the two counties adjudged this liberty to belong to our church. Then the justices who were present enrolled their verdict.

HOW THE ABBOT DISPUTED WITH HIS KNIGHTS

ABBOT SAMSON began a struggle with his knights, he against all and all against him. He declared that they ought to make to him the full service of fifty knights in scutages, aids, and the like, since, as they admitted, they held the fees of that number of knights. He disputed as to why ten of those fifty knights should be free from service, and as to the reason or authority those forty received the service of ten knights. They all with one voice answered that such was his custom, that ten of them should ever help the forty, and they said that on this matter they would neither make answer nor stand trial, as they ought not to do so.

But when they were summoned to make answer on this matter in the court of the king, some craftily excused themselves and others craftily appeared, the latter saying that they ought not to answer without their peers. On another occasion, those who had at first

A.D. 1196.

absented themselves appeared, and said the same thing, that they ought not to make answer without their peers, who were with them in the dispute.

And when they had thus many times mocked the abbot, and had vexed him with great and heavy expenses, the abbot complained on this matter to archbishop Hubert, who was then justiciar. And he answered in the full council that each knight ought to reply for himself and for his own holding. And he said openly that he knew well, and was well able to secure, the right of his church against all and every one of them.

Then earl Roger Bigod was the first to acknowledge freely that in law he owed his lord, the abbot, the full service of three knights, and both in reliefs, and scutages, and aids. But as to the wardenship of the castle of Norwich, he was silent.

After that there came two of the knights, and then three, and then more, and eventually almost all, and, following the example of the earl, admitted the same service. And as a recognition made on this matter in the court of St. Edmund was not enough, the abbot took with him to London at his own expense the wives and women, who were heiresses of lands, that they might make recognition in the king's court, and each received a separate charter.

Alberic de Vere and William de Hastings, and two others were in the service of the king, across the sea, when these things were done, and therefore this dispute had to await final settlement.   Alberic de Vere was the last who resisted the abbot; but the abbot took and sold his cattle, by which means he was driven to come to the court and make answer as his peers had done. And so he took counsel, and at last recognised the right as belonging to St. Edmund and the abbot.

Therefore when all the knights had been overcome, the abbot might have made great gain of money from so notable a victory, had he not desired to spare some of them.   For whenever twenty shillings are charged on a fee, there will remain for the abbot twelve pounds, and if more or less be charged, then more or less will remain, according to the due proportion.   Further, the abbot and his predecessors were wont at the end of twenty weeks to give seven shillings for the wardship of the castle of Norwich from his own money, to supply the defect of the three knights; fees which earl Roger Bigod holds of St. Edmund.   And all the knights of the four constabularies used to pay twenty-eight pence when they began to make wards, and one penny to the marshal who collected those pennies, and they gave twenty-eight pence and no more, because the ten knights of the fifth constabulary were want to assist the other forty. Therefore, when they ought to have given three shillings in full, they gave only nineteen pence, and one who should have entered upon the duty of making ward at the end of four months, entered at the end of twenty weeks. Now, however, all the knights paid three shillings in full, and the amount by which it has been increased beyond twenty-nine pence remains to the abbot, wherefore he can repay himself the said seven shillings.

Thus was seen how the threats of the abbot, which he uttered on his first day when he received the homage of his knights, had their fulfilment, when, as has been related, all the knights promised him twenty shillings and at once went back on their promise, refusing to give him a total sum of more than forty pounds in making aids and performing wards and in all like things.

In Tivetshall there is some land on the fee of the abbot which used to pay to the watchmen of the castle of Norwich waite-fee, which is to say, twenty shillings a year, at the rate of five shillings at each of the four fasting times. This is an ancient custom which the abbot was very anxious to change if he could.　But as he saw his weakness in this matter, he still is silent and conceals his wish.

CONCERNING HENRY OF ESSEX

In order to spread far and wide the memory of the blessed king and martyr, we have added what follows to our writings, not improperly we hope　It is not that I, who am unimportant and almost of no account at all, should put this out with an historical title, but that master Jocelin, our almoner, a man of renowned piety, one mighty in word and deed, at the pressing requests of the powers that be, at last thus began it in this way; and I regard the work as mine, since, according to the precept of Seneca, I may without presumption ascribe to myself whatever has been well said by another.

When the abbot was come to Reading, and we with him, we were rightly received by the monks of that place.　And among them was Henry of Essex as a professed monk, who, when he had a chance to speak to the abbot and to those who were present, told us how he had been conquered in a trial by battle, and how and why St. Edmund confounded him in the very hour of conflict.   But I wrote down his tale by command of the lord abbot, and I wrote it also in these words.

Inasmuch as it is impossible to avoid unknown evil, we have thought it well to commit to writing the acts and crimes of Henry of Essex, that they may be a warning, and not a example.   Stories often convey a useful and salutary warning.

The said Henry, then, while he enjoyed great prosperity, had the reputation of a great man among the nobles of the realm, and he was renowned by birth, noted for his deeds of arms, the standard-bearer of the king, and feared by all men owing to his might.   And when others who lived near him enriched the church of the blessed king and martyr Edmund with goods and rents, he on the contrary not only shut his eyes to this fact, but further violently, and wrongfully, and by injuries took away the annual rent of five shillings, and converted it to his own use.

In the course of time, moreover, when a case arose in the court of St. Edmund concerning a wrong done to a certain maiden, the same Henry came thither, and protested and declared that the trial ought to be held in his court because the place where the said madien was born was within his lordship of Lailand.

With the excuse of this affair, he dared to trouble the court of St. Edmund for a long while with journeyings and countless charges.

But fortune, which had assisted his wishes in these and other like matters, brought upon him a cause for lasting grief, and after mocking him with a happy beginning, planned a sad conclusion for him; for it is the custom of fortune to smile, that she may rage; to flatter, that she may deceive; and to raise up only that she may cast down. For presently there rose against him Robert de Montfort, his relative, and a man not unequal to him in birth and power, and slandered him in the presence of the princes of the land, accusing him of treason to the king. For he asserted that Henry, in the course of the Welsh war, in the difficult pass of Coleshill, had treacherously cast down the standard of the lord king, and proclaimed his death in a loud voice; and that he had induced those who were coming to the help of the king to turn in flight. As a matter of fact, the said Henry of Essex believed that the renowned king Henry the Second, who had been caught in an ambush by the Welsh, had been slain, and this would have been the truth, had not Roger, earl of Clare, a man renowned in birth and more re-

A.D. 1157.

nowned for his deeds of arms, hastened up quickly
with his men of Clare, and raised the standard of the
lord king, which revived the strength and courage of
the whole army.

Then Henry resisted the said Robert in the council,
and utterly denied the charge, so that after a little
while the matter came to a trial by battle. Then
when they met at Reading to fight on
an island somewhat near the abbey,
there gathered there also a multitude
of persons, to see how the affair would end. And it
came to pass, that when Robert manfully made his
armour ring again with hard and frequent blows, and
his bold beginning promised the fruit of victory,
Henry's strength began to fail him a little. And as
he looked round about, behold! on the edge of land
and water, he saw the glorious king and martyr
Edmund, armed and as it were flying in the air, and
looking towards him with an angry countenance, often
shaking his head in a threatening manner, and showing
himself full of wrath. And Henry also saw with the
saint another knight. Gilbert de Cereville, who appeared not only less than the saint in point of dignity,
but also head and shoulders shorter; and he looked on
him with accusing and angry glances. This Gilbert,

A.D.
1163.

by order of the said Henry, afflicted with bonds and tortures, had died, as the result of an accusation brought against him by the wife of Henry, who cast the penalty for her own ill-doing on an innocent man, and said that she could not endure the evil suggestions of the said Gilbert.

When he saw these sights, then, Henry grew alarmed and fearful, and called to mind that an old crime brings new shame. And now, giving up all hope, and abandoning skilful fighting for a blind rush, he took the part of one who attacks rather than that of one who defends himself. And when he gave hard blows, he received harder ; and while he fought manfully, he was more manfully resisted. In a word, he fell conquered.

And as he was thought to be dead, in accordance with the earnest request of the magnates of England, the relatives of the said Henry, the monks of that place were allowed to give burial to his corpse. But he afterwards revived, and when he had regained the blessing of health, under the regular habit, he wiped out the stain of his former life, and taking care to purify the long week of his dissolute past with at least one sabbath, he cultivated the study of virtues, to bring forth the fruit of happiness.

HOW THE ABBOT DECEIVED THE BISHOP OF ELY FOR THE GOOD OF HIS CHURCH

GEOFFERY RIDEL, bishop of Ely, sought from the abbot a supply of wood for making some great buildings at Glemesford, and the abbot granted this request against his will, for he did not at that time dare to offend the bishop. But while the abbot was staying at Melford, a certain clerk of the bishop came and asked on behalf of his lord that they might be allowed to take the said wood at Elmswell; and he made a mistake in his speech, saying Elmswell where he should have said Elmset, the latter being the name of a certain wood at Melford. And the abbot marvelled at the message, for such wood was not to be found at Elmswell.

Then when Richard the forester of the same township had heard this, he told the abbot privately that the bishop in the preceding week had sent his carpenters as spies into the wood of Elmset, and that they had chosen the best trees in the whole wood, and marked them with their signs. At this news, the abbot saw at once that the messenger of the bishop had delivered his message wrongly, and told him that he would gladly meet the wish of the bishop.

On the morrow, after the messenger had departed, as soon as he had heard mass, the abbot went with his carpenters into the said wood, and caused all the oaks which had already been marked, and more than a hundred others, to be marked for the use of St. Edmund, and for the completion of the great tower; and he ordered that they should be cut down as rapidly as possible.

But the bishop, when he learned from the report of his messenger that the needed wood was to be taken at Elmswell, overwhelmed the messenger with much abuse, and sent him back to the abbot that he might correct the word which he had said wrongly, that is, when he said Elmswell for Elmset. But before he had come to the abbot, all the trees, which the bishop desired, and which his carpenters had marked, had been cut down. It was therefore necessary for the bishop to take other trees and in another place, if he would. But I, when I saw this, laughed and said in my heart, "Thus craft is defeated by craft."

HOW THERE WERE DISPUTES CONCERNING THE APPOINTMENT OF BAILIFFS FOR THE TOWN

On the death of abbot Hugh, the wardens of the abbacy desired to depose the bailiffs of the town of

St. Edmund's, and to appoint new
bailiffs by their authority, alleging
that this right pertained to the king,
in whose hand the abbey was.   But when we made
complaint on this matter and sent our messengers to
the lord Ranulf Glanvill, who was then justiciar, he
answered that he was well aware that forty pounds
ought to be rendered from the town to our sacristan
annually, and especially for the lights of the church.
And he added that abbot Hugh, according to his
pleasure and in his chamber, without the assent of
the monastery, had given the office of bailiff as often
and to whomsoever he would, saving the forty pounds
of revenue for the altar ; it was therefore not remark-
able if the officials of the king exacted this right on
the king's behalf.   Then in rough tones, he called all
us monks fools in that we had allowed our abbot to
do such things, nor thinking that the chief duty of
monks is to keep silence, and to shut their eyes to all
the faults of their prelates, nor thinking of the fact
that we are called cheats if in any matter, either
rightly or wrongly, we raise opposition, and that
sometimes we are accused of treason, and sometimes
condemned to imprisonment and exile.   For these
reasons, it seems the wiser counsel to me and those in

my position, rather to die as confessors than as martyrs.

When our messenger returned to us and told what he had heard and seen, we took counsel, as it were unwillingly and under compulsion, to the effect that, by the common action of the monastery and of the wardens of the abbey, the old bailiffs of the town should be deposed; this was as far as possible to be a joint act, though Samson, who was our subsacristan, was opposed to the plan.

At a later date, when he had been made abbot, Samson was not unmindful of the injury which had been done to the abbey, and on the morrow of the Easter next after his election, he caused the knights and clerks and many burgesses to be gathered together in our chapter, and in the presence of all of them said that this town belonged to the monastery and to the altar, especially in the matter of finding lights for the church. And he said that he wished to renew the old custom, that all that concerned the balliwick of the town and such like matters pertaining to the monastery, should be decided in the presence of the monastery and by common assent.

And at the same time two burghers, Godfrey and Nicholas, were named bailiffs, and there was a dispute as to the question from whose hand they should

receive the horn, which is called moot-horn.   At last
they received it from the hand of the prior, who after
the abbot is the chief man in the affairs of the
monastery.   Then those two bailiffs peacefully exer-
cised their jurisdiction for many years, until they
were said to be slack in administering the justice of
the king.   Then at the suggestion of the abbot himself, that greater security might be given to the
monastery in this matter, they were removed, and
the sacristan Hugh received it into his hand.   He
appointed new servants, who were responsible to him
for the balliwick.   In course of time, however—
I know not for what reason—new bailiffs were again
appointed elsewhere than in the chapter, and without
the assent of the monastery, on which account there
was a fear of the same or greater danger after the
death of abbot Samson than there had been after the
death of abbot Hugh.

And one of our brothers, who was fully confident
of the love and friendship of the abbot, took an
opportunity to address the abbot on this matter,
with due modesty, and he declared that the monastery
murmured for this cause.   When the abbot heard
this he was long silent, as if he were somewhat
troubled for this, and at last, so it is said, answered as

follows: "Am not I, even I, the abbot? Is it not
my affair to dispose of the goods of the church committed to my care, provided that I act wisely and
according to God? If there be a default in the
administration of the king's justice in this town,
I shall be accused on the matter, I shall be summoned
to the court, on me will fall the labour of the journey
and the expense, and the defence of the town and of
that which pertains thereto. It will be I who am
regarded as a fool and not the prior or the sacristan
or the monastery. No, it will be I, who am and
ought to be their head. By my means and by my
counsel, with God's help, the town shall be preserved
unharmed so far as in me lies, and the forty pounds
of annual rent to the altar shall be preserved. Let
the brothers murmur; let them blame me; let them
say what they will among themselves. I am their
father and abbot, and while I live, I will not give
mine honour to another."

When he had so spoken, the monk left him and
told his answers. But I marvelled at such words,
and thought the thing over in secret and with care.
At last I was forced to doubt still, since the rule of
law says and teaches us that all things are in the disposition of the abbot.

HOW ABBOT SAMSON DISPUTED WITH THE MEN OF LONDON ABOUT THE PAYMENT OF TOLLS

THE merchants of London wished to be quit from toll at the fair of St. Edmund's. Many, however, though unwillingly and under compulsion, paid it, and on this account, many tumults and a great disturbance occured between the citizens of London in their court. Wherefore, having held a meeting about the matter, they sent word to abbot Samson that they ought to be quit of toll throughout all England, under the authority of the charter which they held from king Henry the Second.

To this the abbot answered that, were it needful, he could easily bring the king to warrant him that he had never made them a charter in prejudice of our church, or to the injury of the liberties of St. Edmund, to whom the holy Edward had granted and confirmed toll and theam and all regalian rights before the conquest of England. And he added that king Henry had given to the Londoners quittance from toll throughout his own demesnes, where he had the right to give it; for in the city of St. Edmund's he could not give it, for it was not his to give.

When the Londoners heard this, they decreed with common assent that none of them should come to the fair of St. Edmund's, and for two years they did absent themselves, whence our fair suffered great loss, and the offerings in our sacristy were greatly diminished. Eventually, when the bishop of London and many others had mediated, an agreement was reached between them and us whereby they should come to the fair, and some of them should pay toll, but this should be at once returned to them, that by such a device the privilege of both parties might be maintained.

But as time went on, when the abbot had come to an agreement with his knights, and as it were rested in peace, lo! again, "The Philistines be upon thee, Samson!"   For the Londoners, with one voice, threatened to level with the earth the stone houses, which the abbot had built in the same year, or to take distress a hundredfold from the men of St. Edmund, if the abbot not at once make reparation to them for the wrong which they had suffered from the bailiffs of the town of St. Edmund's.   For they had taken fifteen pence from the carts of the citizens of London, which were coming from Yarmouth and carrying herrings, and which passed through our town.   And the citizens of London said that they had been quit of toll in every market, and always and in every place, throughout all England, from the time when the city of Rome was first founded, at which time the city of London was also founded.   They said that they ought to have this privilege throughout all England, both on the ground that their city was a privileged city, which had been the metropolis and capital of the kingdom, and on the score of the antiquity of the city.

The abbot, however, asked for a truce on this dispute for a reasonable time, until the return of the king to England, that he might consult with him on this matter; and taking the advice of men skilled in the law, he handed back to the complainants those fifteen pence as a pledge, without prejudice to the question of the right of either party.

HOW THERE WAS A DISPUTE WITH THE BURGHERS AS TO THE DUES FROM THE TOWN

In the tenth year of the abbacy of abbot Samson, by common council of our chapter, we made complaint to the abbot in his court and said that the receipts from all the goods of the towns and boroughs of England were increased, and had grown to the advantage of the

A.D. 1192.

possessors and the greater profit of their lords, save in the case of this town, which had been wont to pay forty pounds and had never had its dues increased. And we said that the burghers of the city were responsible for this, since they held so many and such large stands in the market-place, shops and sheds and stalls without the assent of the monastery, and at the sole gift of the bailiffs of the town, who were annual holders of their offices, and as it were servants of the sacristan, being removable at his good pleasure.

But when the burghers were summoned, they answered that they were under the jurisdiction of the king, and that they ought not to make reply, contrary to the liberty of the town and their charters, concerning that which they had held and their fathers well and in peace, for one year and a day without dispute. And they said that it was the old custom that the bailiffs should, without consulting the monastery, give to them places for shops and sheds in the market-place, in return for some annual payment to the balliwick. But we disputed this, and wished the abbot to dispossess them of such things as they held without having any warrant for them.

Then the abbot came to our council, as if he had been one of ourselves, and privately informed us that he wished, so far as he could, to do right to us ; but that he had to proceed in a judicial manner, and that he could not, without the judgment of the court, dispossess his free men of their lands and revenues, which they had, whether rightly or wrongly, held for many years. He added that if he were to do this, he would be liable to punishment at the discretion of the king and at the assizes of the kingdom.

The burghers, therefore, took council and offered the monastery a revenue of a hundred shillings for the sake of peace, and that they might hold that which they held as they had been accustomed. But we would not grant this, preferring to postpone the matter, and perchance hoping that in the time of another abbot, either we might recover all, or change the place of the fair ; and so the matter for many years advanced no further.

CONCERNING THE CHARTER GRANTED TO THE TOWN BY THE ABBOT

But when the abbot had returned from Germany, the burghers offered him sixty marks, and sought his confirmation of the liberties of the town, under the same form of words as that in which his predecessors

A.D. 1194.

Anselm and Ording and Hugh had confirmed them to them. And this also the abbot graciously conceded. But while we murmured and grumbled, a charter was made for them, as he had promised to them ; and as it would have been a source of shame and confusion to him if he had been unable to do that which he had promised, we would not oppose him, or provoke him to anger. But the burghers, from the time when they had the charter of abbot Samson and the monastery, were full of confidence that they would never lose their holdings and liberties in the time of abbot Samson ; and therefore, never afterwards would they, as they had done before, give or offer the said revenue of a hundred shillings.

The abbot, however, at length turned his attention to this, and assembling the burghers together about the matter, said that if they would not make their peace with the monastery, he would forbid their sheds to be put up at the fair of St. Edmund's. Then they answered that they would give every year a silken cope, or some other ornament to the value of a hundred shillings, as they had before promised. But they offered this on condition that they should be quit for ever from the tenths on their money which the sacristan sternly exacted from them.

The abbot and the sacristan opposed this offer, and so the dispute was again left unsettled. But we have lost those hundred shillings from that day to this, according as is said in the proverb, "He that will not when he may, when he will he shall have nay."

HOW THE MONASTERY WAS TROUBLED WITH INCOMPETENT CELLARERS

CELLARERS succeeded each other in rapid succession, and each one of them at the end of the year was oppressed with great debt. The twenty pounds from Mildenhall were given to assist the cellarer, and proved insufficient. Afterwards there were assigned to him forty pounds a year from the same manor, and still the cellarer said that this was not enough.

Accordingly the abbot, wishing to provide for his own safety and comfort and for ours, as he knew that in the case of any deficiency we must appeal to him, as the father of the monastery, associated with our cellarer one of the clerks of his table, master Ranulf by name, that he might assist him as a witness and companion both in the paying out and in the receiving of money.

And behold! there was much diversity of opinion. Murmurs rose; lies were invented; slanders are joined to slanders, nor is there a spot in the house which is not resounding with poisonous hissings. One says to another, "What is this which has been done? Who has seen such things? Never was such a disgrace inflicted on a monastery. See! the abbot has made a clerk superior to a monk. See! he has made a clerk master and guardian over the cellarer, that he may be able to do no good without him. The abbot little regards his monks; he suspects them: he consults the clerks; he love clerks. How is the gold become dim! how is the most fine gold changed!"

And friend said to friend, "We are become a reproach to our neighbours. All we monks are held to be either dishonest or extravagant; credit is given to a clerk, not to a monk; the abbot has more confidence in a clerk than in a monk. Why should this clerk be more faithful, or wiser, than some monk?" And one said to his companion, "Are not our cellarer and sub-cellarer, or cannot they be, as faithful men as the sacristan or as the chamberlain? The result is that this abbot or his successor will associate a clerk with the sacristan, and a clerk with the chamberlain, and a clerk with the subsacristans, to collect the offerings at the shrine, and so with all the officials, whereby we shall become a laughing-stock and a scorn to all people."

But when I heard these things, I used to answer, "If I were cellarer, I should wish to have a clerk to be my witness in all that had to be done, and so if I did well, he would bear witness of the good, but if at the end of the year I were burdened with any debt, I should be able by means of the clerk to gain credence and be excused."

I heard a certain one of our brothers, a man discreet and learned indeed, say a thing which moved me and many others. "It is not wonderful," he declared, "if the lord abbot intervenes in matters connected with the safe conduct of our affairs. For he rules wisely the part of the abbey, which belongs to him, and he makes wise dispositions for his house; and it is his concern to supply that which is lacking to us, if a want arises owing to our carelessness or poverty. But," he continued, "there is yet one possible danger which may arise after the death of abbot Samson, and such a danger has never been in all the days of our life. There is no doubt that the officers of the king will come and will take the abbey into his hand, that is, the barony which pertains to the abbot, as has been done hitherto, after the death of other abbots, and as was done before on the death of abbot Hugh, the officials of the king will desire to appoint new bailiffs in the town of St. Edmund, alleging as their authority that abbot Hugh did this. And for the same reason, in course of time, the officials of the king will appoint a clerk of theirs to watch over the cellar, that all things may be done through him and by his command, and they will say that this ought to be done because abbot Samson did so. And in this way

A.D.
1109-12.

they will be able to mingle and to confound the affairs and revenues of the abbot and of the monastery, which abbot Robert, of happy memory, after taking counsel, separated and divided from each other." And when I heard these and other like words from a man of great wisdom and prudence, I was overwhelmed and was silent, wishing not to condemn and wishing not to excuse the lord abbot in so great a matter.

HOW THE ABBOT RESISTED HUBERT WALTER WHEN HE CLAIMED LEGATINE AUTHORITY OVER THE ABBEY

HUBERT WALTER, archbishop of Canterbury, and legate of the apostolic see and justiciar of England,

ABOUT
A.D. 1198.

after he had visited many churches, and had changed many things and introduced innovations by his legatine authority, on his return from his carnal mother, who was dying at Dereham where she dwelt, he sent to us two of his clerks, who bore sealed letters from their lord, in which it was announced that we should give credence to their sayings and acts. Then these clerks made enquiry of the abbot and monastery as to whether we would receive their lord, the legate, who was coming to us, in such a manner as a legate ought to be received, and as he had been received in other churches. And if we would grant this, then he would shortly come to us, to settle the business and affairs of our church according to God, with the advice of the abbot and monastery. But if we would not grant this, those two clerks would explain to us more in detail the message of their lord.

Then the abbot summoned the majority of the monastery and we took counsel that we should give a favourable answer to the clerks who had been sent to us, saying that we would receive their lord, as legate, with all honour and respect, and that we should send with them our messengers, who should say the same to the lord legate on our behalf. And our idea was that, as we had previously done in the case of the bishop of Ely and other legates, we should show him all honour with a procession and the ringing of bells, and receive him with the other due ceremonies, until perchance he should come to hold a visitation in the chapter. And if he wished to do this, then at last we should all resist him in common to the face, appealing to Rome and trusting to our charters.

The lord abbot said also, "If the legate now wishes to come to us, let us act in this manner as has been said. But if he delay his coming to us for a while, let us again seek counsel of the lord pope, and ask what force the privileges of our church, which we have obtained from him and his predecessors, ought to have as against the archbishop, who has obtained power from the apostolic see over all the other privileged churches of England." Such then was our counsel.

And when the archbishop heard that we would receive him as legate, he received our messengers graciously, and with giving of thanks. And he became kind and friendly to the lord abbot in all his affairs, and delayed his coming among us for a while on account of some urgent business. Therefore, without any delay the abbot sent to the lord pope the same letters which the legate had sent to the monastery, which announced that he would come to us by the authority of his legation and by the authority of the lord pope, and in which it was written that power had been given him over all the exempt churches of England, notwithstanding letters granted to the church of York and others.

So at the instance of the messenger of the abbot, the lord pope wrote to the lord of Canterbury and declared that our church, his spiritual daughter, was accountable to no legate, unless it might be to a legate *a latere*, sent by the lord pope, and forbade him to stretch forth his hand over us. And the lord pope added, on his own account, that he further forbade him to exercise power over any other exempt church. Our messenger returned to us and the matter was hidden for some days. But it was made known to the lord of Canterbury by his friends in the court of the lord pope.

Now when at the end of the year the legate made his visitation in Norfolk and Suffolk, and had come first to Colchester, he sent a secret messenger to the abbot, and informed him that he had heard it said many times that the abbot had obtained letters against his legation, and asked that he would send those letters to him in a friendly way. And so it was done, for the abbot had two copies of the letters

in identical terms.   But the abbot visited the legate
neither in person nor through any intermediary, as
long as he was in the bishopric of Norwich, lest he
might be thought to desire to come to terms with the
legate as to the matter of providing entertainment for
him, as the other monks and canonical persons had
done.   The legate, for his part, was disturbed and
angry, and fearing that he would be shut out if he
should come to us, passed through Norwich, Acre,
and Dereham to Ely, making his way towards London.

Then within a month, the abbot appeared before
the legate between Waltham and London, in the
king's highway, and the legate blamed him because he
would not come to him as justiciar of the lord king,
when he was in that district.   But the abbot answered
that he had been there not as justiciar, but as legate,
making scrutiny in all churches, and brought forward
as his excuse the season of the year, and that the Passion
of the Lord drew near, at which time it was necessary
for him to be engaged in divine services and in the
observances of the cloister.   And when the abbot met
words with words and objections with objections, and
could not be terrified or bent, the legate answered with
anger that he well knew that he was skilled in argument,
and that he was a better clerk than the legate was.

Therefore the abbot, without passing over in a cowardly manner things which ought not to be mentioned, or speaking arrogantly of those things which had to be said, in the audience of many men, answered that he was the type of man who would never allow the liberty of his church to be infringed, either owing to lack of knowledge or to lack of money, even if it were necessary for him to die or be condemned to perpetual banishment. And when an end was made of these and other like altercations, the legate began to blush when the abbot spoke softly and prayed that he would deal more mildly with the church of St. Edmund, for the sake of his native land, for he was as it were a son of St. Edmund and there brought up. He blushed, indeed, because he had thoughtlessly poured forth the poison which he had conceived within him.

On the morrow, word was brought to the archbishop of Canterbury that the lord of York was coming to England as legate, and that he had hinted many evil things to the lord pope concerning him, saying that he had oppressed the churches of England by taking on account of his visitation thirty thousand marks of silver. For that reason the legate sent his clerks to

A.D.
1199.

the abbot, asking that he would write with the other abbots to the lord pope and defend him. And then the abbot granted this, and gave witness that the lord of Canterbury had neither come to our church, nor oppressed that or any other church, speaking according to his knowledge. And when the abbot had handed over those letters to the messengers of the archbishop, he said before all men that he had no fear even if the archbishop wished to make an improper use of these letters. And the clerks answered on the peril of their master's soul, that their lord wished not to deal craftily, but only desired to excuse himself. And so the archbishop and the abbot were made friends.

HOW THE ABBOT CONTENDED WITH HIS KNIGHTS AS TO SERVICE ACROSS THE SEA

KING RICHARD sent orders to all the bishops and abbots of England that every nine knights should furnish a tent, and that these should come to him in Normandy without delay, with horses and arms, to help him against the king of France. It therefore was

A.D.
1198.

necessary for the abbot to be responsible for the sending of four knights. And when he had caused all his knights to be summoned, and had gathered them together on this matter, they answered that their fees, which they held of St. Edmund, were not liable to this, and that neither they, nor their fathers, had ever gone out of England, though they had sometimes paid scutage by command of the king.

Then the abbot was in a difficult position, as on the one hand he saw that the liberty of his knights was endangered, and on the other feared lest he might lose seisin of his barony for default of service to the king, as had happened to the bishop of London and to many barons of England. And he at once crossed the sea, and having wearied himself with many labours and expenses and with the many presents which he gave to the king, at first he was unable to come to terms with the king by means of a money payment. And so, when the king said that he needed neither gold nor silver, but instantly demanded the four knights, the abbot offered him four mercenary knights. And the king received these and sent them to the castle of Eu. And the abbot gave them thirty-six marks at once for their expenses for forty days.

But on the morrow there came certain friends of the king, and counselled the abbot that he should proceed cautiously, saying that the war might last for a full year or more, and the cost of the knights increase and multiply to the perpetual loss of him and his church. They therefore advised that before he left the court, he should come to terms with the king, so that he might be quit of the said knights after forty days. Then the abbot, taking good advice, gave a hundred pounds to the king for this quittance, and so returned to England in high favour with his lord. And he bore with him the king's writ that distraint should be levied on the fees of his knights to repay him for the service which he had made to the king on their behalf.

When the knights were summoned, they alleged their poverty and many different grievances, and offered their lord two marks from each fee. And the abbot, not unmindful of the fact that he had himself burdened them in that same year, and had brought a suit against them to force them to pay a full scutage, wished to win back their favour, and graciously accepted that which they willingly offered to him.

At that time, though the abbot incurred great expenses over sea, he did not return empty-handed to

his church, but brought with him a golden cross and
a precious copy of the scriptures, which was worth
twenty-four marks.   And on another occasion, when
he had returned from across the sea, sitting in his
chapter he said that had he been cellarer or chamberlain he would have sought for something which
would be helpful in the administration of his office.
And he added that as he was abbot he ought to
acquire something which was fitting for an abbot,
and saying this he offered the monastery a costly
chasuble and a mitre inlaid with gold, and sandals
with silken buskins, and the head of a pastoral staff,
made of silver and well worked.   In the same way,
as often as he returned from beyond the sea, he
brought some ornament with him.

HOW THE ABBOT TOOK CHARGE OF THE CELLAR, AND HOW FOR THAT CAUSE MURMURING AROSE IN THE MONASTERY

In the year of grace one thousand one hundred and
ninety-seven, certain changes and alterations were
made in our church, which may not be
passed over in silence.   When our
cellarer did not find his ancient
revenues sufficient, abbot Samson ordered that fifty

A.D.
1197.

pounds should be given him in annual increase from Mildenhall by the hand of the prior. This was not to be paid at one time, but in instalments every month, that in each month there might be something to spend, and that the whole might not be used up in one part of the year; and so it was done for one year.

But the cellarer and his assistants complained of this, and he said that if he had had that money in his hands, he would have provided for himself and gathered stock for himself. Then the abbot, against his will indeed, granted that request. And when the beginning of August came, the cellarer had already spent the whole amount, and moreover owed twenty-six pounds, and was bound to pay a debt of fifty pounds before Michaelmas.

And when the abbot heard this, he was wroth, and spoke thus in the chapter, " I have often threatened that I would take our cellar into my own hands owing to your incompetence and extravagance, since you bind yourselves with great debt. I placed my clerk with your cellarer as a witness, that the office might be managed with greater care. But there is no clerk or monk who dares tell me the cause of the debt. It is said, indeed, that the too elaborate feasts in the prior's house, which occur with the assent of the prior and of the cellarer, and the superfluous expense in the guest-house owing to the carelessness of the guest-master, are the cause of it. You see," he went on, "the great debt which is pressing on us ; tell me your opinion as to the way in which the matter should be remedied."

Many of the cloistered monks, hearing this, and, as it were, laughing to themselves, were pleased with what was said, and said privately that what the abbot said was true. The prior cast the blame on the cellarer, and the cellarer on the guest-master, and the guest-master made excuse for himself. We, of course, knew the true reason, but were silent from fear. On the morrow the abbot came and again said to the monastery, "Give me your advice as to how your cellar may be more thoughtfully and better managed." And there was no one who would answer a word, save one who said that there was no waste at all in the refectory whence any debt or burden could arise. And on the third day the abbot said the same words, and one answered, "The advice ought to come from you, as from our head."

Then the abbot said, "Since you will not give advice, and cannot rule your house for yourselves, the control of the monastery falls upon me as your father and chief guardian. I receive," he went on, "into my own hand your cellar and the charge of the guests, and the task of getting supplies within and without." And with these words, he deposed the cellarer and guest-master, and replaced them with two monks, with the titles of sub-cellarer and guest-master, and associated with them a clerk of his table, master G., without whose assent nothing was to be done in the matter of food and drink, or in expenditure or in receipts. The former buyers were removed from the work of buying in the market, and food was to be purchased by a clerk of the abbot, and our deficits were to be made good from the abbot's treasury. Guests who ought to be received were received, and those who ought to be honoured were honoured. Officials and cloistered monks alike took their meals in the refectory, and on all sides superfluous expenses were cut down.

But some of the cloistered monks said among themselves, "There were seven, yes, seven, who devoured our goods, and if one had spoken of their devouring, he would have been regarded as one guilty of high treason." Another said, as he stretched forth his hands to heaven, "Blessed be God, Who hath given such a desire to the abbot, that he should correct so great faults." And many said that it was well done.

Others said that it was not well done, thinking so great a reformation derogatory to the honour of the house, and calling the discretion of the abbot the ravening of a wolf; and in truth they called to mind old dreams, to the effect that he who should become abbot would raven as a wolf.

The knights were astonished, the people marvelled, at these things which had been done, and one of the common sort said, "It is a strange thing that the monks, being so many and learned men, should allow their affairs and revenues to be confused and mingled with the affairs of the abbot, when they had always been wont to be separated and parted asunder. It is strange that they do not guard themselves against the danger which will come after the death of the abbot, if the lord king should find things in this state."

A certain man again said that the abbot was the only one who was skilled in external affairs, and that he ought to rule all, who knew how to rule all. And one there was who said, "If there were but one wise monk in so great a monastery, who might know how to rule the house, the abbot would not have done such things." And so we became a scorn and derision to those who were round about us.

About this time it happened that the anniversary of

abbot Robert was to be celebrated in the chapter, and
it was decreed that a Placebo and a Dirige should be
sung more solemnly than was wont, that is, with ringing of the great bells, as on the anniversaries of abbots
Ording and Hugh.   The cause of this was the noble
deed of the said abbot Robert, who separated our
goods and revenues from those of the abbot.   But this
solemnity was due to the counsel of some that so the
heart of the lord abbot might be moved to do well.
One there was, however, who thought that this was
to be done to the shame of the abbot, who was accused
of wishing to confound and intermingle his affairs and
revenues and ours, in that he had taken our cellar into
his own hand.

Then when the abbot heard the unusual ringing of
bells, and knew well and considered that this was contrary to custom, he wisely hid the cause of the action
and sang mass solemnly.   But on the following
Michaelmas, since he wished to silence the murmurs
of some men in part, he appointed him who had been
sub-cellarer to the post of cellarer, and ordered another
to be nominated as sub-cellarer, though the same clerk
remained with them and procured all needful things
as before.   But when that clerk passed the bounds of
moderation, saying, " I am Bu,"—whereby he meant

that the cellarer had passed the bounds of temperance in drinking,—and when, without consulting the abbot, he held the court of the cellarer and took sureties and pledges, and received the revenues for the year and spent them with his own hand, he was publicly called chief cellarer by the people.

And when the clerk often wandered through the court, and many poor and rich debtors followed him as if he had been master and chief agent, as well as claimants of divers sorts and on divers matters, perchance one of our officials stood in the court. He saw this, and wept for shame and confusion, thinking that this was a shame to our church, and thinking of the danger which would result, and thinking that a clerk was preferred to a monk to the prejudice of the whole monastery. Accordingly he, whoever he was, procured by means of another, that this should be fitly and moderately pointed out to the lord abbot, and it came to pass that it was brought to the abbot's knowledge how arrogant the clerk was, and what he did to the shame and wrong of all; and that he was the cause of great disturbance and discord in the monastery. But when the abbot heard this, he at once ordered word to be sent to the cellarer and to the said clerk, and commanded that the cellarer should henceforth regard himself as cellarer in the receipt of money, and in holding pleas, and in all other matters, saving this only, that the said clerk should assist him, not on an equality, but as a witness and adviser.

CONCERNING THE WILL OF HAMO BLUND

HAMO BLUND, one of the richest men of that town, being on his death-bed, was scarce willing to make any will. At length, however, he left three marks by will, no one hearing his wishes except his brother and his wife and a chaplain. And when the abbot held an inquest after his death, he summoned those three and sternly rebuked them because the brother, who was the heir, and the wife, would not permit any other to come to the sick man, desiring to gain all things.

And the abbot said in full audience, "I was his bishop, and I had the care of his soul; that the ignorance of his priest and confessor may not be harmful, and because I was absent and could not advise the sick man while he yet lived, it is my concern that I should do so even when it is late. I command that all his money and moveable property, which is reported to be worth two hundred marks, shall be written down, and that one portion shall be given to the heir, and a second to his wife, and a third to his poor relations and to other poor men. But the horse, which was led before the coffin of the dead man, and which was offered to St. Edmund, I order to be sent back and returned. For it is not right that our church should be disgraced by the present of him who died intestate, and who is accused by report of having been wont often to lend his money upon usury. By the face of God, if what has now happened occur again in the case of any man in my time, he shall not be buried in the cemetery." And when he had so spoken, the others went away in confusion.

HOW THERE WERE RIOTS IN THE CEMETERY, AND CONCERNING THAT WHICH WAS DONE IN THE MATTER

On the morrow of the Nativity of the Lord, meetings and sports and bandying of words were held in the cemetery between the servants of the abbot and the burghers of the town; and from words it came to blows, from blows to wounds, and to bloodshed. But when the abbot knew of this, he privately called together some of those who had come to the spectacle, but who had taken no part in it, and commanded the names of all the offenders to be written down. And he caused all of them to be summoned to appear to make answer before him in the chapel of St. Denis on the morrow of the feast of St. Thomas the archbishop. And in the meantime he would not invite any of the burghers to his table, as he had been wont to do in the first five days of Christmastide.

So on the appointed day, when oath had been taken from sixteen legal men, and their evidence had been heard, the abbot said, " It is well known that those wrong-doers have broken the canon *Latae sententiae*. But as there are laymen in both parties, and they know not how great a crime is such notable sacrilege, that the others might fear the more I will excommunicate them by name and publicly, and that justice may not be in any wise lacking, I will begin with my domestics and servants."

Then this was done, when we had robed and lighted the candles. And all went out from the church, and having taken counsel, they all stripped themselves, and, naked except for their underclothes, prostrated themselves before the door of the church. And when the assessors of the abbot had come, monks and clerks, they told him in lamentable tones that more than a hundred men lay thus naked, and the abbot was grieved. Yet showing the rigour of the law in his word and face, and concealing the kindness of his heart, he wished to be compelled by his advisers to absolve the penitents, knowing that mercy should be exalted against judgment, and that the church should receive all penitents. Therefore all were heavily scourged and absolved, and all swore that they would abide by the judgment of the church for the sacrilege which had been done.

But next day a penance was assigned to them according to the provisions of the canons, and so the abbot received all in full peace, and threatened terrible things to all who in word or deed should produce cause for dispute. Then also he publicly forbade meetings and spectacles to be held in the cemetery, and so, when everything had been restored to peace, the burghers ate with the lord abbot on the days following with great joy.

HOW THE MONKS WERE RESTORED TO COVENTRY

A commission of the lord pope was issued to Hubert, archbishop of Canterbury, and the lord bishop of

A.D.
1197.

Lincoln, and to Samson, abbot of St. Edmund's, for the reformation of the church of Coventry and for the restoration of the monks, without hearing the case again. And so the parties to the suit met at Oxford, and the judges received letters from the lord king, asking that the matter might be postponed. Then the archbishop and the bishop dissembled and kept silence, and as it were sought the favour of the clerks. But the abbot alone spoke openly as a monk for the monks of Coventry, publicly favouring their case and defending them. And by his means, it advanced so far on that day that a certain simple seisin was made to one of the monks of Coventry to the value of one pound. But the restoration of the whole body was for a while delayed, that to this extent at least the abbot might meet the request of the lord king.

At the time fourteen monks of Coventry, who were present there, were entertained by the abbot in his lodging, and while the monks were seated at table in one part of the house, and the masters of the schools, who had been invited, the abbot was praised as being magnanimous and magnificent in his entertainment, nor was he ever in his life seen in better spirits than then, owing to his zeal for the reform of the monastic order.

And when the next feast of St. Hilary came, the abbot went with great gladness to Coventry, and was overcome neither by labour nor by his expenses, and he said that if he had to be borne in a horse litter, he still would not tarry. Then he came to Coventry, and for five days waited for the archbishop, and honourably maintained all the said monks with their servants, until a new prior was created and the monks solemnly introduced into the church. He who has ears to hear, let him hear; the deed is worthy of remembrance.

A.D. 1198.
13TH JANUARY.

18TH JANUARY.

HOW THE ABBOT ENDOWED SCHOOLS AT SAINT EDMUND'S

AFTER these things an agreement was made between abbot Samson and Robert de Scales as to the half of the advowson of the church of Wetherden, and the same Robert acknowledged the right of St. Edmund and of the abbot. The abbot, when no agreement had

A.D.
1198.

been made beforehand, and no promise had been given, gave the half of that church which belonged to him to master Roger de Scales, brother of the same knight, on condition that he would render an annual pension of three marks by the hand of our sacristan to the master of the schools, who should read in the town of St. Edmund's.

The abbot was led to do this by motives of memorable generosity, and since he had already bought stone houses for the purposes of the school that the poor clerks might be quit from house rent, so henceforth they were free from all exaction of money, which the master of the schools had, according to custom, exacted for their education. Then by the will of God and in the lifetime of the abbot, the whole half of that church, which was worth, so it is said, a hundred shillings, was turned to such uses.

CONCERNING IMPROVEMENTS WHICH THE ABBOT MADE IN THE ABBEY

Now when the abbot had built many different buildings in his townships throughout the abbacy, and had taken up his residence on them more often and more frequently than with us at home, at last he returned, as it were, to himself. And making good, as it were,

better, he said that he would stay at home more than
had been his wont, and that he would build houses
which were needed, regarding things within and
without, and knowing that the presence of the master
is the profit of the field.

Accordingly he ordered that the stables and offices
in and around the court, which had previously been
covered with reeds, should be covered with new roofs,
made of slates, by means of Hugh the sacristan, that so
all fear might be removed and all danger of fire.   And
behold the acceptable time, the day which had been
desired !   Of this I cannot write without joy, for that
I had the care of the guests.   Behold ! by order of
the abbot, the court resounded with spades and with
the tools of masons, that the guest-house might be
overthrown, and now was almost entirely razed,
since the Highest planned its restoration !

The abbot built a new larder for himself in his
court, and gave the old larder of the monastery for the
use of the chamberlain, since it was unfittingly situated
under the dormitory.   The chapels of St. Andrew and
St. Catherine and St. Faith were newly covered with
lead.   And many improvements were effected within
and without the church.   If you do not believe, open
your eyes and behold !

And in his time also our stone almonry was constructed, which had before been out of repair and built of wood, and to the cost of this one of our brothers, Walter the physician, who was then almoner, contributed that which he had made from the practice of medicine.

Moreover, when the abbot saw that the silver table of the high altar, and many other precious ornaments, had been alienated for the recovery of Mildenhall and for the ransom of king Richard, he would not restore that table or other similar things, which for a like purpose might be torn away and distrained. But he turned his attention to the construction of a most valuable crest over the shrine of the glorious martyr Edmund, that his ornament might be placed there, whence for no reason could it be taken away, and where no man would dare to lay hands upon it. Indeed, when king Richard was taken captive in Germany, there was no treasure in England which was not given or for which redemption was not made, yet the shrine of St. Edmund remained intact.

For when there was a dispute before the justices in the exchequer court as to whether the shrine of St. Edmund should be partially dismantled for the ransom of the king, the abbot arose and said, " Know it for the truth that this shall never be done by me, nor is there any man who can compel me to assent to this. But I will open the doors of the church; let him enter who will, let him approach who dares." And all the justices answered with oaths, "I will not come near it," "I will not come near it." And they said, "St. Edmund is even more angered against those who are far away and absent, than he is with those who are present and would take away his cloak." And when this had been said, the shrine was not stripped, nor was a ransom paid for it. And for this cause the abbot omitted other things, and turned his mind with forethought and providence to the making of a crest for the shrine. And now the plates of gold and silver resounded between the hammer and the anvil, and the smiths worked with their tools.

HOW THE ABBOT DISPUTED WITH THE KING AS TO THE WARDSHIP OF THE LAND OF ADAM DE COKEFIELD

ADAM DE COKEFIELD died, and left a daughter of three months as his heir, and the abbot gave the ward-ship of the fief to whomsoever he would. But king Richard, at the request of some of his friends, earnestly

ABOUT
A.D. 1198.

sought the wardship and the child for the advantage of a servant of his own, both by letters and by messengers. But the abbot replied that he had given the wardship, and had confirmed the gift under his charter; and sending a messenger to the king, tempted him with prayers and presents, that he might so calm his wrath.

Then the king answered with great anger that he would avenge himself on the proud abbot, who opposed him, if he were not ready to refrain from his reverence for St. Edmund whom he feared. Therefore the messenger of the abbot returned, and the abbot wisely concealed the threats of the king, and said, " Let the king send if he will, and take possession of the wardship ; he has force and power to perform his will, and to take away the whole abbacy. I will never bend to do readily that which he desires, and it shall never be done by my means. For there is fear that such an action might be drawn into a precedent to the hurt of my successors, and for this matter I will never give the king money. Let the Most High regard it. I will bear patiently whatever may befall."

Then when many said and believed that the king was moved against the abbot, lo ! the king wrote in a friendly way to the abbot, and sent word that he should present to him some of his dogs. And the abbot was mindful of the saying of a wise man, "Presents, believe me, move both men and gods, and Jupiter himself may be appeased with gifts." So he sent the dogs for which the king asked to him, and in addition he sent also horses and other valuable gifts. And when the king had graciously received these, he commended the uprightness of the abbot and his fidelity to his trust publicly in the presence of his earls and barons, and sent to the abbot in token of his friendship and love a valuable ring, which the lord pope Innocent the Third had given him for his great affection to him, and which was the first gift which had been made to him after his coronation. And he sent many things by his writ to him for the presents which he had sent.

HOW THE CUSTOMARY DUES OF THE TOWN WERE CHANGED

MANY marvelled at the changes in the customary dues which took place with the orders or consent of the lord abbot Samson. From the time when the town of St. Edmund's received the name and liberty of a borough, the men of every house had been wont to give to the cellarer one penny at the beginning of August for the reaping of our corn, which tax was called rep-selver. And before the town was free all were wont to reap as slaves, and only the houses of the knights and chaplains and servants of the court were free from this tax. But as time passed, the cellarer spared some of the richer men of the town and exacted nothing from them.

When the other burghers saw this, they said publicly that no one who had a messuage of his own ought to pay that penny, but only those who rented the houses of others. Afterwards, all in common sought this freedom, coming to the lord abbot about it, and offering an annual payment in place of this exaction. Then the abbot learnt that the cellarer had gone through the town to collect rep-selver in a wrongful manner, and that he had caused sureties to be taken from the houses of the poor men, taking sometimes tripods, and at others doors, and other goods, and how the old women appeared with their distaffs, threatening and cursing the cellarer and his men. And he decreed that twenty shillings should be given to the cellarer every year at the next portman-moot, by the hand of the bailiff, before

August, by the burghers who should give money to pay this.

And this was done, and confirmed by our charter. And they were given quittance from a certain customary due which is called sor-penny, in return for four shillings to be paid at the same time. For the cellarer had been wont to receive one penny a year for each cow, belonging to the men of the city, which went out to pasture, unless the cows were those of the chaplains or servants of the court, and these cows he used to put in the pound, and about this he used to have much trouble.

But later on, when the abbot spoke of this in the chapter, the monastery was indignant and angry, and so Benedict, the sub-prior made answer for all in the chapter, and said, "He, that abbot Ording, who lies there, would not have done such a thing for five hundred marks of silver." But the abbot was angry at this, and postponed the matter for a time.

CONCERNING A DISPUTE BETWEEN THE CELLARER AND THE SACRISTAN

ALSO a dispute arose between Roger the cellarer and Hugh the sacristan concerning the perquisites of their offices, so that the sacristan would not lend to the cellarer the prison in the town for the imprisonment of robbers, who were taken in the fee of the cellarer. Wherefore the cellarer was often vexed, and when the robbers escaped, was blamed for the failure of justice.

But it happened that a certain free tenant of the cellarer who remained without the gate, a man called Ketel, being accused of robbery and defeated in a trial by battle, was hanged. And the monastery was grieved at the abusive words of the burghers, who said that if the man had lived within the gate, the matter would not have come to trial by battle, but that he would have been acquitted by the oaths of his neighbours, as was the privilege of those who dwelt within the borough.

And when the abbot and the more reasonable section of the monastery saw this, and observed that the men, both without and within the borough are our men, and that all should enjoy the same liberty within the jurisdiction of the abbey, except the villeins adscript to the soil at Hardwick and their like, provided with care that this should be so.

Then the abbot being anxious to define with definite conditions the offices of the cellarer and of

the sacristan, and to calm disputes, as though he
favoured the side of the sacristan, gave orders that the
servants of the bailiff of the town and the servants of
the cellarer should enter together the fee of the
cellarer to take robbers and malefactors. And he
ordered that the bailiff should have half the pay due
for the imprisonment and guarding of the men and
for the labour required, and that the court of the
cellarer should go to the portman-moot, and that
there cases which had to be adjudged should be
adjudged with common assent. And it was also
resolved that the men of the cellarer should go the
toll-house with the rest, and there renew their sureties, and that they should be inscribed in the roll of
the bailiff, and pay a penny to the bailiff there, which
payment is called borth-selver, and that the cellarer
should have half of it. Now, however, the cellarer
receives nothing on this account.

All this was done that all might enjoy equal liberty.
But the burghers still say that those who dwell without the town ought not to be free from market toll,
unless they are members of the gild merchant.
And the bailiff, with the assent of the abbot, claims
the pleas and forfeitures of the fee of the cellarer to
this day.

CONCERNING THE CUSTOMS AND DUES
OF THE CELLARER

THE old customs of the cellarer, which we have seen, were as follows:—The cellarer had a messuage and barns near Scurun's well. There he was wont to hold his court solemnly for the trial of robbers and all other pleas and disputes. There he used to place his men in pledge and enrol them, and to renew the pledges every year, and to take for this such money as the bailiff took at the portman-moot. This messuage, with the garden adjoining it, which a tenant holds now, was the manor of Beodric, who was formerly lord of that town, and the town was therefore formerly called Beodricsworth, and his demesne lands are now in the demesne of the cellarer. That which is now called averland was the land of his villeins. The total amount of his holding and those of his men was thirty times thirty acres of land, and these are still the fields of the town. The service from this, when the town was made free, was divided into two parts, so that the sacristan or bailiff might receive a free tax of twopence from each acre. The cellarer was to have the ploughing and other services, that is, the ploughing of one rood for every acre without giving of food, and this custom is still observed.

He was also to have the folds where all the men of the town, with the exception of the steward, who has his own fold, were bound to place their sheep, and this custom is still observed. And he was to have also ave-penny, that is twopence for every thirty acres, but this custom was changed before the death of abbot Hugh, when Gilbert de Elveden was cellarer.

The men of the town, by order of the cellarer, were wont to go to Lakenheath, and to bring back a catch of eels from Southrey, and often they returned empty handed, so that they were burdened without profit to the cellarer, wherefore it was ageed among them that henceforth every thirty acres of land should pay one penny a year, and the men remain at home. That land, however, is now so divided that it is hard to tell what rent should be paid from it, with the result that I have seen the cellarer in one year take twenty-seven pence, while now he can hardly take tenpence halfpenny.

Again, the cellarer used to have authority in the roads without the town, so that no one was permitted to dig for chalk or clay without a licence from him. And he used to summon the fullers of the town, that they should give cloth for his chalk. Otherwise, he would prohibit them the use of water, and would take the webs which he found there, and these customs still maintain. And also whoever bought of the cellarer corn or anything, used to be free from toll at the gate when he went out, for which cause the cellarer sold his goods at a higher price, and this custom still remains. Also the cellarer was wont to take toll from flax, when it was carried about, at the rate of one bundle from each load. And the cellarer alone ought, and used, to have a free bull in the fields of this town; now more men have free bulls. And whenever any one gave his land held in burgage in frank almoin to the monastery, and this was handed over to the cellarer or to another official, that land was wont to be quit from haggovele, and especially when it was assigned to the cellarer, on account of the importance of his office, for that he is the second father in the monastery, and for respect to the monastery, since the state of those who procure our food ought to be good. This custom the abbot regards as unjust, since the sacristan loses his service.

The cellarer was also wont to warrant the servants of the court, that they should be free from scot and tallage, but now this is not the case, for the burghers say that the servants of the court ought to be quit indeed as far as they are servants, but not in so far as they hold land in burgage in the town, and in so far as they or their wives buy or sell publicly in the market. The cellarer was wont to take all the manure in every street for his use, except such as was before the doors of those who had averland; for they alone might collect and have it. That custom rather fell into abeyance in the time of abbot Hugh, until Dennis and Roger de Henghem were cellarers. They, wishing to revive the ancient custom, seized the manure carts of the burghers, and caused them to be unloaded. But as a number of burghers then resisted successfully, every one now collects the manure which is on his holding, and the poor sell theirs when and to whom they will.

The cellarer had also this right in the market of the town, that he and his agents should buy first in the case of all food for the use of the monastery, if the abbot were not at home. The buyers of the abbot or of the cellarer, whichever should come first to the market, was to buy first, either the former without the latter, or the latter without the former; in case they both came at the same time, the preference was given to the abbot's agents. At the time when herrings were sold, the abbot's agents were always to buy a hundred herrings for a penny less than other men, and

the cellarer and his agents had the same right.   If a
load of fish or other food should come first to the
court or should come into the market, and the load
had not been taken from the horse or from the cart,
then the cellarer and his agents might buy and take
for themselves the whole load without toll.   Abbot
Samson, however, ordered his agents that they should
give place to the cellarer and his agents, because, as he
himself said, he would rather that he lost than his
monastery.   Accordingly, the agents, in honour preferring one another, when anything came to be sold
which was not enough for both parties, bought the
thing jointly and divided it equally, and so discord
became concord between the head and the members,
and between the father and his sons.

HOW THE AUTHOR WAS BLAMED FOR PRAISING THE ABBOT TOO MUCH

THE poet has said that envy aims at the highest,
and so I relate that when a certain person saw the
present writing, and read of so many good actions, he
called me a flatterer of the abbot, and said that I was
hunting after grace and favour, telling me that I had
passed over in silence some things which ought not to

have been left unmentioned. And when I asked him
what things, and what sort of things these were, he
answered, " Have you not seen that the abbot gives
the escheated lands in the demesnes of the monastery,
and heiresses of lands being minors, and widows both
within and without the town of St. Edmund's, to
whomsoever he will? Have you not seen that the
abbot has attracted to himself suits and pleas of those
who by royal writ claim lands which are of the fee
of the monastery and more especially suits in which
there is money to be gained ; and that he passes on
those suits in which there is no profit to the cellarer
or the sacristan or the other officials ?"

And to this I answered as best I knew how, and
perhaps well, perhaps ill, saying that every lord of a
fief, to whom homage is due, ought to have the escheat
by law, when there is one in the fief, whence he receives homage ; and for a similar reason, ought to
have a general aid from the burghers and the wardship of boys, and marriage rights over widows and
girls, in those fees whence he has homage ; and all
these things seemed to belong to the abbot alone,
unless by chance the abbacy should be vacant. In the
town of St. Edmund's, however, as it is a borough,
there is a custom that the wardship of a boy, until he

comes to years of discretion, and his inheritance, vests with the nearest relative.

And as to suits and pleas, I answered that I had never seen the abbot ursurp to himself our pleas, unless on account of a failure of justice on our part; but yet that he had sometimes received money that, by the intervention of his authority, suits and pleas might come to a right conclusion. And I have sometimes seen pleas, which belonged to us, conducted in the abbot's court, since there was no one who at the beginning of the case would claim the trial for the monastery.

HOW THERE WAS A FIRE NEAR THE SHRINE OF SAINT EDMUND

In the year of grace one thousand one hundred and ninety-eight, the glorious martyr Edmund willed to terrify our monastery, and to teach us that his body should be more reverently and carefully guarded. There was a certain wooden floor between the shrine and the high altar, on which were two candles, which the guardians of the shrine used to relight. And they were wont to put one candle on another, and to

A.D. 1198.

stick them together carelessly.   And under this floor
many things were lying together in an untidy manner,
such as flax and thread and wax and vessels of different
sorts, in fact the keepers of the shrine used to put
there whatever came into their hands, behind the
door with iron sides which the place had.

On the night of St. Etheldreda's day then the
keepers were asleep, and part of a candle, which had
been relit, fell, as we believe, while it was still burn-
ing, on the same floor which was covered with rags.
And it caught all things which were near it, and
those above and underneath went on fire, so that the
iron walls were all white hot.   And lo! the anger of
the Lord was kindled, but not without mercy, as it is
written, In wrath remember mercy.   For in the
same hour the clock struck before the hour of matins,
and the master of the vestry arose and perceived and
knew of the fire.   Then he ran at once, and sounding
the gong, as if for a dead man, he cried with a loud
voice and said that the shrine was on fire.

Then we all ran up and found the fire raging with
incredible fierceness, and surrounding the whole
shrine, and almost reaching the beams of the church.
Then the young men ran for water, some to the well
and some to the clock, and some used their hoods,

and with great labour put out the fire. But first they stripped some of the altars. Then, when cold water had been poured on the front of the shrine, the stones fell and were reduced as it were to dust. And the nails with which the silver plates were fastened to the shrine came out of the wood, which had been burnt to the depth of my finger, and the plates hung one from another without nails.

Yet the golden image of the saint at the front of the shrine, and some stones, remained firm and unharmed, and the image was more beautiful after the fire than it had been before, because it was of pure gold.

Now it happened by the will of the Most High, that at this time the great beam, which had been over the altar, had been taken away that it might be newly carved. It happened also that the cross, and the little Mary, and the John, and the chest with the garment of St. Edmund, and the case containing the relics, which had formerly hung from the same beam, and other holy things which had stood on the beam, had all been carried away beforehand. Otherwise, we believe that they would all have been burnt, as a painted cloth was burnt, which was hanging in the place of the beam. But what would have happened if the church had been hung with curtains?

So when we were sure that the fire had nowhere entered the shrine, after carefully looking at the cracks and chinks, wherever they were, and after seeing that all was cold, our sorrow was greatly lessened. And lo! some of our brothers cried with much wailing that the cup of St. Edmund was consumed. And when many sought the stones and metal plates in all directions among the ashes and cinders, they brought forth the cup quite unharmed. It was lying in the midst of a heap of ashes, which were now cool, and it was found covered with a linen cloth, which, however, was half-burned. The oak chest, also, in which the cup was usually placed, had been burnt to ashes, and only the iron fastenings and the iron lock were found. Then when we saw this miracle, we all wept for joy.

Then when we saw that the greater part of the front of the shrine had been ruined, and were angered at the wickedness of the cause of the fire, with common assent a goldsmith was privately summoned, and we caused him to make plates and fix on the shrine without any delay, that the scandal might be avoided, and we caused the signs of the fire to be covered up with wax or in some other way.

But the gospel bears witness, There is nothing hid which shall not be revealed. Very early in the morning there came strangers bearing gifts, and noticed nothing of the fire. Yet some of them looking round, asked where the fire round the shrine had been, of which they had already heard. And so when it was impossible to conceal it altogether, we answered those who asked that a candle had fallen and burnt three napkins, and that owing to the heat of the fire some stones on the front of the shrine had been destroyed. Yet lying rumour pretended that the head of the saint had been burnt; some said that only the hair had been consumed; but in the end the truth was known, and the mouth of them that spoke lies was stopped.

Now all this was done, by the providence of the Lord, that the places round the shrine of His saint might be more honestly cared for, and that that which the lord abbot proposed might the more quickly come and without delay come to a fitting conclusion. For he proposed that the shrine, with the body of the glorious martyr, should be placed more securely and splendidly in a more prominent position. And, before this same misfortune befell, the crest of the shrine was half finished, and the marble stones for raising and supporting the shrine had been largely prepared and polished.

HOW THE ABBOT ATTRIBUTED THE FIRE TO THE GREED OF THE MONKS

THE lord abbot, who was absent, was greatly grieved when he heard these rumours. And on his return home, he came into the chapter and said that these and other like perils would result from our sins, and especially because of our murmuring about our food and drink. And he turned the blame to some degree rather on the whole monastery than on the avarice and carelessness of the guardians of the shrine.

Therefore, that he might skilfully lead us to abstain from our pittances, at least for one year, and that we might appropriate the revenues of the pittancy to the restoration of the shrine with pure gold, he gave the first example of generosity himself. For in our presence, he gave the whole treasure in gold, which he had, that is, fifteen golden rings of the value, it is believed, of sixty marks, towards the restoration of the shrine. And we all granted that our pittances should be given for this purpose, until our decision was changed by the sacristan, who said that St. Edmund was well able without such assistance to repair his own shrine.

CONCERNING THE DREAM THAT A CER-
TAIN GREAT PERSON HAD, AND HOW
THE ABBOT INTERPRETED THE SAME

AT this time some great person, I know not who it
was, came and told a vision of his to the abbot,
whereby the abbot was much moved, and related it in
full chapter with a very bitter speech. And he told it
in this way : "That is a true vision," he said, "which
a certain great man has seen. For he beheld the
holy martyr Edmund lying without his shrine, and
saying with groans that he was robbed of his garments and wasted with hunger and thirst, and that
his cemetery and the halls of his church are carelessly
guarded."

And the abbot interpreted this dream in the
presence of all, turning the blame on us in this way :
"St. Edmund declares that he is naked because you
withheld your old clothes from the naked poor, and
give unwillingly that which you ought to give, and
do the same in the matter of food and drink. The
idleness, the neglect of the sacristan and his fellows,
is very clear from the recent disaster of the fire which
has occurred between the shrine and the altar."

HOW THE MONKS INTERPRETED THE DREAM IN A DIFFERENT WAY, AND HOW THEY ANGERED THE ABBOT ON THAT ACCOUNT

AT these words the monastery was grieved, and after the chapter many of the brothers met together and interpreted the dream in this way : " We are the naked limbs of St. Edmund," they said, "and the monastery is his naked body. For we have been despoiled of our ancient customary dues and liberties. The abbot has all things ; the chamberlainship, the the sacristy, the cellar. And we perish with hunger and thirst, when we cannot have our food save by means of a clerk of the abbot and through his ministration. If the guardians of the shrine were negligent, the abbot may put it down to himself, for he it was who appointed such men." And in this way many spoke in the monastery.

But when this interpretation was made known to the abbot, as he was in the forest of Harlow on his way back from London, he was very wroth and greatly moved, and he answered and said, "They would turn that dream against me. By the face of God! as soon as I shall reach home, I will restore to them what they call their customary dues, and I will take my clerk away from the cellarer, and I will leave them to their own devices. And at the end of the year I shall see how wise they are. For this year I have stayed at home, and I have caused their cellar to be supplied without debt. And they show such gratitude towards me!"

And so when he returned home, and was intending to translate the holy martyr he humbled himself before God and men, thinking that he would amend his way in all things, and make peace with all men, and especially with his monastery. Then as he sat in the chapter he ordered a cellarer and subcellarer to be chosen by our common assent; and he removed his clerk, saying that whatever he had done, he had done for our welfare, calling to witness God and His saints, and excusing himself in many ways.

CONCERNING THE TRANSLATION OF THE BODY OF SAINT EDMUND

HEAR, O Heaven, the things which I speak; give ear, O earth, to the deed of abbot Samson. For, when the feast of St. Edmund drew nigh, A.D. 1198. 20TH NOVEMBER. the marble stones were polished, and all things were made ready for the elevation of the shrine. Accordingly, the feast was celebrated on a Friday, and on the following Sunday a three days' fast was proclaimed to the people, and the cause for that fast was publicly announced. Moreover, the abbot preached to the people that they should prepare themselves for the transference of the shrine and for placing it upon the high altar, until the masons should have completed their preparations. And he appointed a time and method for so great a work.

Therefore, when we had on that night come to the time of matins, the great shrine stood upon the altar empty within, adorned with white doe-skins, and one panel stood below against a pillar of the church, and the holy body lay still where it was wont to lie. Then hymns of praise were sung, and we all went to take our discipline. After that, the lord abbot and some with him were clothed in white raiment, and approaching with reverence, as was right, hastened to uncover the coffin.

Now there was a linen cloth outside, which covered the coffin and all the other things, and which was found to be fastened with some strings of its own. Next there was a silken cloth, and then another linen cloth, and then a third, and so at last the coffin was uncovered and stood upon a wooden stand, that the coffin might not be harmed by the marble stone.

Above the breast of the martyr, and on the outside of the coffin there lay a golden angel of the length of a man's foot, having a golden sword in one hand and a standard in the other. And beneath it was a hole in the coffin's cover, where the former guardians of the martyr were wont to put in their hands to touch the holy body. And there was this verse written over the image:

Lo! the image of St. Michael keeps the martyr's corpse.

And there were iron rings at the two ends of the coffin, as there used to be in Danish chests.

Therefore raising the coffin with the body, they bore it to the altar, and I gave my sinful hand to help in the carrying, though the abbot had ordered that no one should approach unless he were summoned. And the coffin was enclosed in the shrine, the panel being put in place and shut up.

Now we all thought that the abbot would show the coffin to the people in the octave of the feast, and would have the holy body translated in the presence of all men; but we were quite deceived, as that which followed proved. On the Wednesday, while the monastery was chanting compline, the abbot

spoke with the sacristan and Walter the physician,
and having taken counsel, summoned twelve brothers,
who were strong to bear the panels of the shrine, and
were skilled in fastening and unfastening them.   And
the abbot said that he had prayed to see his patron
saint, and that he wished that the sacristan and
Walter the physician should be joined with him in
making the inspection.   And the two chaplains of
the abbot were named, and the two guardians of the
shrine, and the two masters of the vestry, and six
others, the sacristan Hugh, Walter the physician,
Augustine, William de Diss, Robert and Richard.

So while the monastery slept, those twelve dressed
in white drew the coffin from the shrine, and bore it
and placed it on a table near the old place of the
shrine.   And they prepared themselves to remove
the cover, which was joined and fastened to the
coffin was sixteen very long iron nails.   And when
they had with difficulty done this, all were ordered
to stand afar off, save the two associates above mentioned.

Now the coffin was filled with the holy body, and
that both in respect of its length and of its breadth, so
that it was hardly possible for a needle to be placed
between the head and the wood, or between the feet

and the wood. And the head lay joined to the body, being a little raised by a small pillar.

And so the abbot looking near, found after this a silken cloth which covered the whole body, and then a linen cloth of wonderful whiteness; and over the head a little linen cloth, and another small and skilfully made silken cloth, as it were the veil of some holy woman. And then they found the body wrapped in a linen cloth, and so at last all the lines of the holy body were clearly traceable.

Here the abbot stopped, saying that he dared not go further, and behold the naked body of the saint. Therefore, he held his head between his hands, and said with a groan, "Glorious martyr, holy Edmund, blessed be that hour in the which you were born. Glorious martyr, turn not my daring to my hurt, in that I, who am a sinner and wretched, touch you. You know my devotion and my intention." And then he touched the eyes and nose, the latter being thick and very large, and afterwards touched the breast and arms, and raising the left hand touched the fingers and placed his own fingers between those of the saint. And going further he found the feet standing upright as though they had been the feet of a man but lately dead, and he touched the toes, and counted them as he touched them.

And then counsel was taken that other brothers should be summoned and behold these miraculous things, and six came upon summons, and six other brothers who forced their way in without the assent of the abbot, and these saw the holy body. Their names were Walter de St. Alban's, Hugh the farmer, Gilbert the prior's brother, Richard de Hengham, Jocell the cellarer, and Thurstan the Little; and the last alone put forth his hand and touched the feet and knees of the saint. And, that there might be abundance of witnesses, by the disposition of the Highest, one of our brothers, John de Diss, sat on the roof of the church with the servants of the vestry, and saw all these things plainly.

After these things had been done, the cover was fastened on the coffin with the same nails as before, and with the same number and in the same manner, and the martyr was covered with the same cloths and those in the same order, as he had first been found. And then the coffin was placed in its accustomed place, and on the coffin, near the angel, there was placed a certain silken bag, in which a document, written in English, was put, setting forth certain salutations of Aylwin the monk, as it is said, and this document was before found near the golden angel when the coffin was uncovered.

And by order of the abbot another little writing was also made, and hidden in the same bag, and the words of this second writing were as follows. "In the year of the incarnation of the Lord one thousand one hundred and ninety-eight, abbot Samson, being led by devotion, saw and touched the body of St. Edmund, on the night next after the feast of St. Catherine, in the presence of these witnesses,"— and there were written below the names of the eighteen monks.

Then the brothers wrapped the whole coffin in a sufficiently large linen cloth, and placed above it a valuable new silken cloth, which Hubert, archbishop of Canterbury, had sent as an offering in the same year, and they placed a certain double linen cloth of the same length as the coffin next the stone, that neither the coffin nor the wooden platform on which it rested might be injured by the stone. After this the panels were brought up and fitly joined together in the shrine.

And when the monastery came to chant matins, and saw these things, all who had not seen the body were grieved, and said among themselves, "We have been grossly deceived." But when the hours of matins had been chanted, the abbot called the monas-

tery before the high altar, and having briefly explained
to them that which had been done, declared that it
was neither right nor possible to summon them all to
such events. And on hearing this, we sang, "Te
Deum laudamas" with tears, and hastened to ring
the bells in the choir.

Four days later the abbot deposed the guardians of
the shrine, and the guardian of the shrine of St.
Botolph, and he appointed new guardians for whom
he laid down rules, that they might take more honest
and diligent care of the sanctuaries. And the great
altar, up to this time, was concave, and on it things
were often placed with little reverence. This space
and that which was between the shrine and the altar,
he caused to be filled up with stone and cement, that
there might be no danger of fire possible for the
negligence of the guardians, as had been the case
before, according to that which a wise man says,
Happy is he whom the perils of others make cautious.

HOW KING JOHN VISITED THE ABBEY
SOON AFTER HIS ACCESSION

WHEN the abbot had purchased the favour and
grace of king Richard with gifts and money, so that

he believed that he could carry through all his affairs according to his desire, king Richard died, and the abbot lost his labour and expenditure. But king John after his coronation laying aside all his other work, at once came to St. Edmund's, being led to do so by his vow and devotion. And we thought that he would have made some great offering, but he offered a silken cloth, which his servants borrowed from our sacristan and have not yet paid for.

He enjoyed the hospitality of St. Edmund, which involved great expenses, and when he left he gave nothing at all honourable or beneficial to the saint, except thirteen pence sterling, which he paid for a mass for himself, on the day on which he departed from us.

CONCERNING THE DISPUTE BETWEEN THE PORTER AND THE MONKS

At that time some of our officials complained and said in the chapter that Ralph the porter, our servant, appeared in cases and suits against them to the injury of the church and to the prejudice of the monastery. The prior commanded, with the common assent of the monastery, that he should be punished according to our custom by which our servants were wont to be punished, that is by the confiscation of their incomes.

Therefore orders were given that the cellarer should withdraw from him, not the salary which of right pertained to his office, according to the witness of his charter, but certain additions and grants which the cellarer and subcellarer had made to him, without the assent of the monastery. But the same Ralph, taking with him certain of those of the table of the abbot, complained to the abbot on his return from London, that the prior and the monastery had deprived him of his salary, of which he was possessed when the abbot first came into the abbacy. And they told the abbot that this was done without him, and to his shame, and unreasonably, when he was not consulted and the case was not tried.

Then the abbot believed this, and was moved more than was right or usual with him, and constantly excusing Ralph and protesting that he was innocent, came into the chapter. And making complaint on this matter, he said that what was done, was done to his prejudice, since he was not consulted. Then one answered, all the rest supporting him, that this had been done by the prior and with the assent of the whole chapter.

Thereupon the abbot was confused, and said, "I have nourished and brought up children, and they have rebelled against me." And passing over nothing, as he should have done for the peace of the multitude, but rather showing his power, and not allowing himself to be overcome, he publicly commanded the cellarer that he should fully and completely restore all things which had been taken away to the said Ralph, and that he should drink nothing but water until he had restored all things.

Bnt when Jocell the cellarer heard this, he chose rather to drink water on that day, than to returñ Ralph his salary contrary to the will of the monastery. And when the abbot learnt this, on the morrow he forbade the cellarer to eat or drink until he had made complete restitution. And having spoken thus, the abbot at once left the town, and absented himself for eight days.

HOW DISTURBANCES AROSE IN THE MONASTERY, AND OF THE END TO WHICH THEY CAME

ON the day of the abbot's departure, the cellarer arose in the chapter, and showing the command of the abbot, and holding his keys in his hand, said that he would rather be deposed from his office than do anything against the monastery. And there arose a great disturbance in the monastery, such as I never saw before; and they said that the command of the abbot ought not to be observed. But the older and wiser men of the monastery, who wisely kept silence, at last declared that obedience was due to the abbot in all things, unless they were clearly against God, and they agreed in declaring that we must bear with this evil doing for a time and for the sake of peace, lest worst should befal us.

And when the prior had begun to chant the Verba Mea for the dead, as was the custom, the novices resisted, and with them almost half the monastery, and with a loud voice they disputed and opposed him. Yet the older half of the monastery prevailed, though they were few in number as compared with the multitude on the other side.

Now the abbot, being absent, frightened some by his threatening messages, and won over some with his graciousness, and he caused the chief men to abandon the views of the whole body, as though they feared his garments. And so the gospel was fulfilled, "Every kingdom divided against itself is brought to desolation."

And the abbot said that he would in nowise come among us, owing to our conspiracies and the oaths which, as he said, we had taken against him, that we would kill him with our knives.

Then he returned home and sat in his chamber. And he sent word to one of our brothers, who was greatly suspected by him, that he should come to him, and because he would not come, as fearing that he would be taken and bound, he was excommunicated, and for a whole day afterwards he was placed in bonds and remained until morning in the infirmary. The abbot bound three others with a smaller sentence, that the rest might fear.

Next day counsel was taken to summon the abbot and to humble ourselves before him in word and gesture, whereby his mind might be calmed, and so it was done. Then he answered with some humility, but always justifying himself and blaming us, and when he saw that we were ready to be conquered, he was overcome. And with many tears, he swore that he had never been so grieved for anything as for this matter, both for his own sake and for ours, and especially for the evil report, which had already spread abroad our dissension, and which said that the monks of St. Edmund wished to slay their abbot.

Then when the abbot had also told how he absented himself of intent until his anger should have cooled, and repeated the word of the philosopher, I would not have taken vengeance on you, unless I had been angry, he arose with tears and received all and every one of us with the kiss of peace. He wept, and we wept with him. Forthwith the excommunicated brothers were absolved, and thus the storm ceased and there was a great calm.

Yet the abbot secretly ordered that the accustomed salary should be given to Ralph the porter as before and in full. This we passed over, at last realising that there is no lord who does not wish to rule, and that it is a dangerous battle to strive against the stronger and to undertake a contest with the more powerful.

CONCERNING THE KNIGHTS OF SAINT EDMUND AND THEIR FIEFS

In the year of grace one thousand and two hundred, an account of the knights of St. Edmund and of their fiefs was made, of which their ancestors had been possessed.

A.D. 1200.

Alberic de Vere holds five knights and half a knight; that is, in Loddon, and in Brome, one knight; in Mendham and Preston, one knight; in Rede, one knight; and in Cokefield, half a knight; and in Livermere, two knights.

William de Hastings holds five knights; namely, in Lidgate and in Blunham and in Harling the fees of three knights, and in Tibenham and Gissing, two.

Earl Roger holds three knights in Nortune and Brisingeham.

Robert FitzRoger holds the fee of one knight in Marlesford.

Alexander de Kirby holds the fee of one knight in Kirkby.

Roger de Eu holds the fees of two knights in Mickfield and in Topescroft.

Arnald de Charneles and his partners, one knight in Oakley and in Quiddenham, and in Thurston and Stuston.

Osbert de Wachesham, one knight in Marlingford and Wortham.

William de Tostock, one knight in Randeston.

Gilbert FitzRalph, three knights; namely, in Thelmetham and Hepworth one knight; in Reydon, in Blithing, and in Gissing one knight, and in Saxham one knight.

Radulf de Bukenham, half a knight in Old Bukenham.

William de Berdewell two knights in Barningham, and in Berdewell, and in Hunston, and in Stanton.

Robert de Langetot holds three knights, in Stowlangtoft and in Ashfield, in Troston, and in Little Waltham in Essex.

Adam de Cokefield, two knights, namely, in Lavenham and in Onehouse one knight, and in Lilesey.

Robert FitzWalter, one knight in Great Fakenham and in Sapeston.

William Blund, one knight in Thorp.

Gilbert de Peche, two knights, namely in Waude and in Gedding one knight, and in Falsham and Euston and Groton one knight.

Gilbert de St. Clare, two knights in Bradfield and Wattisfield.

Geoffrey de Whelnetham and Gilbert de Manston, one knight in Whelnetham and in Manston.

Hubert de Ansty, half a knight in Briddinghoe.

Gervase de Rothing, one knight in Chipley and in Rothing.

Robert de Halstede, one knight in Halstede and half a knight in Brockley.

Reginald de Brockley, one knight in Brockley.

Simon de Patteshall, half a knight in Whatefield.

Peter FitzAlan, half a knight in Brockley.

Ralph de Pressenei, half a knight in Stanningfield.

Richard de Ickworth, two knights in Ickworth and in Wangford.

Robert de Horning, half a knight in Horningsherth.

Walter de Saxham, one knight in Ashfield and Saxham.

William de Wordwell, half a knight in Whelnetham.

Norman de Risby, half a knight in Risby.

Peter de Livermere and Alan de Flemetun, one knight in Livermere and Ampton.

Roger de Muriaux, one knight in Thorp.

Hugh de Eleigh, two knights in Eleigh and Preston and Bradfield.

Stephen de Brockdish, a fourth of one knight in Brockdish.

Adam de Barningham, a fourth of one knight in Barningham.

William de Wordwell, a fourth of one knight in Livermere and Wordwell.

CONCERNING THE MANORS OF GEOF-
FREY RUFFUS, AND THE CELLAR

GEOFFREY RUFFUS, our monk, though he lived in rather too secular a manner, was of use to us in the custody of four manors, Barton, Pakenham, Rougham, and Bradfield, where there had often in former times been a deficiency in rent. But when the abbot heard ill reports of his morals, for a long while he concealed the matter, perchance because Geoffrey was clearly useful to the whole community. At last, when the truth was known, he suddenly caused his chests to be taken and placed in the vestry, and all the stock of the manors to be strictly guarded, and placed the said Geoffrey in the cloister. There was found a great store of gold and silver to the value of two hundred marks, and all of this the abbot decreed should be devoted to the building of the front of the shrine of St. Edmund.

And when Michaelmas came it was decided in the chapter that two brothers, and not one alone, should succeed to the custody of the manors. Of these one was Roger de Hengham, who publicly promised that he would as well as he could take charge both of the manors and the cellar, and the abbot assented to this, though the monastery was unwilling. Jocell, the cellarer, was then deposed. He had well and providently managed his office, and had controlled the cellar for two years, without contracting debt, contrary to the custom of the other cellarers. And he was made subcellarer. But at the end of the year Roger rendered an account of his receipts and expenses, and declared that he had received sixty marks from the stock of the manors to supplement the deficit of the cellarer.

Therefore, when counsel had been taken, the said Jocell was replaced at the cellar, and Mildenhall, and Chebenhall, and Southwold, and other manors were entrusted to Roger and Albinus, and were separated from the cellar, that neither the manors might be destroyed for the sake of the cellar, nor the cellar destroyed for the sake of the manors

CONCERNING THAT WHICH OCCURRED ON THE DEATH OF ADAM DE COKEFIELD

WHEN Adam de Cokefield was dead, the abbot could have taken three hundred marks for the wardship of the only daughter of Adam ; but as the grandfather of the maid had secretly removed her, and the abbot could not obtain possession of her person, save with the help of the archbishop, he granted that wardship to Hubert, archbishop of Canterbury, on receipt of a hundred pounds.

The archbishop, when he had received five hundred marks, granted that wardship to Thomas de Burgh, brother of the chamberlain of the king, and the maiden was given to him with her right by the hand of the abbot.   Thomas then at once sought seisin of three manors, which had been in our hand after the death of Adam, Cokefield, Semere and Groton.   We thought that we could retain them all in our demesne, or at least two of them—Semere and Groton, both because Robert de Cokefield on his deathbed had publicly declared that he claimed no hereditary right in those two manors, and because his son Adam in full court had acknowledged our right to those two manors and had given his charter on the point, wherein it was laid down that he held those two manors, by the grace of the monastery, for his life only.

When Thomas, then, sought a writ of recognition on the matter, he caused the knights to be summoned to come to make oath before the king at Tewkesbury. Our charters read in public had no weight, for the whole court was against us.   And when oath had been made, the knights said that they knew nothing of our charters, or of private agreements; but they said that they believed that Adam and his father and grandfather for a hundred years back had held the manors in fee-farm, and each after the other, on the days when they were alive and dead. So we were disseised by the judgment of the court after undergoing many labours and many expenses, though the old annual payments of rent were preserved.

HOW THE ABBOT RECEIVED THE ABBOT OF CLUNY

THE lord abbot seemed to be deceived by some appearance of right, because the scripture truly says, I will not give my glory to another. For when the abbot of Cluny came to us, and was received by us as was fitting, our abbot would not give place to him, either in the chapter or in the procession which took place on the Sunday, but sat and stood between the abbot of Cluny and the abbot of Chertsey. And upon this there were different opinions, and many said many things.

A.D.
1200.

HOW ROBERT THE PRIOR DIED, AND OF THE DISCUSSIONS AS TO HIS SUCCESSOR

WHILE Robert the prior was ill and still lived, there was much talk as to the appointment of a new

prior.   Then one said that the lord abbot, sitting in
the choir and beholding all the brothers, from the
first to the last, had not found anyone on whom his
spirit might rest to make him prior, save Heribert his
chaplain.   By these and other like things the will of
the abbot was made clear to many.   And on hearing
this, another answered that this was incredible ; he
asserted that the abbot, a man diligent and provident,
would never give the office of a prior to such a man,
who was a youth and almost a beardless novice twelve
years before, who had only been a cloistered monk for
four years, and who was not proved in the rule of
souls.

Then when the prior was dead, the abbot was in
London, and one said, "A month has not yet passed
since the abbot made Heribert chaplain and subsacristan, and when he gave that post to him in the
chapel of St. Nicasius, he did so with a promise that
if it were in any way possible to make him prior, he
would devote all his care to doing so."   Another
heard this, and wishing to please the abbot and him
who was to be prior, made request to many, both old
and young, that when opportunity was given they
would nominate Heribert, at least in conjunction
with others, for the office of prior.   And he swore

that in this way they would please the abbot, for such was his will.

And there were, indeed, many both among the older and among the younger men, who asserted that the same Heribert was an amiable and affable man, and worthy of great honour. And there were others also, few indeed in number, but more praised in counsel and from the wiser section of the monastery, who wished for master Hermer, the subprior, a mature man, learned and eloquent, skilled and experienced in the rule of souls, who had then ruled the cloister with success for fourteen years an approved subprior and one known. They wished, I say, that he might be preferred to the post of prior, according to the word of wisdom, Trust an experienced master. But the multitude secretly murmured to the contrary, saying that he was a man of ill temper, impatient, restless, turbulent, nervous, litigious, a disturber of the peace. And they mocked him, saying that " the wisdom of a man appears in his patience."

One also said, " There is this one thing which, as it is a scandal, must be greatly feared, that the subprior being removed, learned clerks may not condescend to receive the garb of religion among us, if perchance it happen that some dumb idol be raised up, and a wooden log preferred in so great a monastery. And the same brother added that such a man should be prior of our monastery that, if any matter connected with some great question of ecclesiastical or secular business arose, while the abbot was absent, it might be referred to the prior as to one who was the highest and most discreet member.

When he heard these and other like sayings, one of the brothers said, "Why is it that you multiply so many and such words? When the abbot shall come home he will do what he wills on this matter. Perchance he will seek counsel from all of us and that privately and with much solemnity; but eventually, by arguments and plausible reasonings and twisting words, he will at last reach the fulfilment of his will. And as he has beforehand decided, so will the matter go."

HOW HERIBERT WAS ELECTED PRIOR

THEN the abbot returned and as he sat in the chapter, he put forward many things with sufficient eloquence as to the type of man who ought to be made prior. And John the third prior answered, in the presence of all, that the subprior was worthy, and a suitable person. But at once the multitude cried out, saying, "Give us a man of peace, a man of peace." And two of us answered so great a multitude, and said that such a man ought to be appointed as knew how to rule souls, and to discern between leprosy and leprosy; and this speech was very displeasing since it seemed to favour the party of the subprior.

But the abbot, hearing this tumult, said that he would, after chapter, hear the advice of all men, that so he might proceed wisely in the matter, and on the morrow would settle the affair as he would. And meanwhile one said that the abbot was proceeding with this ceremony that he might cautiously prevent the subprior from obtaining the office of prior, but as if this had been done by the advice of the monastery, and not by the will of the abbot, and that the abbot himself might be held as excused. By this art the mouth of them that speak lies should be stopped.

When the morrow came, the abbot sat in the chapter and wept bitterly. And he said that he had not slept all that night, owing to his anxiety and fear lest he might nominate someone who should not be pleasing to God; and he swore on the peril of his soul that he would nominate four of us, who according to his opinion were the most fitted and suitable, that we might choose one of the four. Then the

abbot named first the sacrist, of whom he knew
well that he was a weak and incompetent man, as the
sacristan himself witnessed with an oath.   And at
once before us all he named John the third prior, his
relative, and Maurice his chaplain, and the said
Heribert, all of whom were full young, about forty
years old or less, and all of moderate intelligence, and
men who needed to learn, rather than to teach, the
rule of souls, though they were ready to learn.

The abbot nominated these three and put them
forward, and he passsd over the subprior and many
other of the senior monks, who were older, more
experienced, learned, and who included those who
had formerly been masters of schools, and all the
others.   Then the abbot spoke at length and highly
commended the person of John, but yet put forward
also the opposite opinion, saying that the number of
his relatives in this district would be a weight round
his neck if he were made prior.

And as the abbot was ready to say the same of
Maurice, as he could do, and thus craftily proceed to
the mention of Heribert, his speech was interrupted,
one of the older men of the monastery saying,
"Master precentor, it is yours to speak first; nominate
lord Heribert."   Then the precentor said, "He is

a good man." And when he heard the name of Heribert, the abbot ceased speaking, and turning to the precentor said, " I will readily receive Heribert, if it is your wish."

At these words the whole monastery cried out, " He is a good man ; he is a good man and lovable." And many of the older men witnessed this same thing, and at once the precentor and some friend with him, and two others from the other side, rose with all haste and placed Heribert in the midst.

But Heribert at first humbly begged to be excused, saying that he was unable to support so great an office, and especially as he said, because he was not so well instructed as to be able to preach in the chapter, as the prior ought to do. Many were amazed when they saw such things, and were dumb with confusion.

But the abbot said much to console him and as it were, in prejudice of learned men, saying that he was well able to remember and consider the sermons of others, as others did. And he condemned rhetorical colouring and elaborate verbiage, and neatly turned sentences in a sermon, saying that in many churches the sermon is delivered in French, or rather in English, for the securing of the improvement of manners, and not as a literary exercise. And when he had so spoken, the newly received prior went to the feet of the abbot, and kissed them. But the abbot received him with tears, and placed him with his own hand in the prior's stall, and commanded all that they should show him due reverence and obedience as their prior.

HOW THE AUTHOR REFLECTED ON THE CHOICE OF HERIBERT

When the chapter was ended, I was sitting as guest-master in the porch of the guest-house, and I was amazed and revolved in my mind that which I had seen and heard. And I began to think subtly for what reason and for what special merits, such a man deserved to be promoted to so great a position. And I began to reflect that he was a man of comely stature and personal appearance, that he was a handsome man and had a kindly face; that he was always cheerful, and showed a smiling face early and late, and friendly to all men; that he was quiet in his manner, sober in his walk, polite in speech, with a sweet voice for chanting and good for reading. I reflected that he was young, strong, and sound in health, and fitted to labour for the needs of the church; that he knew how to suit himself to place and time, at one moment to laymen, at another to clerks, at another to

the regular clergy, and at another to the secular men ;
that he was liberal, sociable, and facile ; that he was
not spiteful in punishing, nor suspicious, nor greedy,
not tiring, not lazy. I reflected that he was sober,
and a fluent speaker in the French tongue, as he was
a Norman by birth ; that he was a man of fair intelligence, who, if learning would not drive him mad,
at least could be called a man of absolute probity.

And when I thought on these things, I said in my
heart, that such a man would be popular, but that
nothing is altogether blessed. And I wept for joy,
saying that the Lord hath visited us, and as it pleased
the Lord, so it had came to pass. But suddenly another thought came to me, " Praise a new man
sparingly, for honours change manners, or rather
make them known. Wait and see first whom and
what manner of men he has as his advisers, and whom
he trusts, for everything naturally draws towards its
like. The event will prove that which has been
done, and therefore I will praise with caution."

HOW THE UNLEARNED BROTHERS MOCKED THOSE THAT WERE LEARNED

On the same day some unlearned brothers, both
officials and cloistered monks, assembled and sharpened

their tongues like a sword that they might privily shoot at the learned. And repeating the words of the abbot which he had on the same day spoken, as if in prejudice of the learned, they said amongst themselves, "Now let our philosophers take to their philosophy; now one can see clearly how their philosophy profits them! Our good clerks have declined so often in the cloister that they are all declined. They have sermonised so much in the chapter, that they are all rejected. They have spoken so often about distinguishing between leprosy and leprosy, that they are now put forth as lepers. They have declined *musa, musae* so often, that they are all reckoned as fools."

These and like words did some put forth in mockery of others and to their shame, and were pleased with their own folly. They abused knowledge of letters, and disparaged those who were learned, rejoicing greatly and hoping great things which perchance will never come to pass, for, Hope of good is ofttimes falsified.

HOW THE ABBOT WAS NOT PERFECT

A wise man has said that no one is altogether blessed, and so abbot Samson was not. This indeed

1 will say, that, in my opinion, he is not to be commended in that which he did when he ordered a charter to be drawn up and to be given to a certain servant of his, that he might have the sergeanty of John Ruffus, after the death of the said John. Ten marks, as has been said, blinded the eyes of the wise.

Master Dennis, also, our monk, speaking of this matter, said that it was a thing unheard of, and the abbot answered, "I will not cease to do my will for you, any more than I would do for that boy there." And the abbot did the same thing in the case of the sergeanty of Adam the farmer, and received a hundred shillings. Of such an act one may say that a little leaven leaveneth the whole lump.

CONCERNING THE FISHPONDS OF BABWELL

There is also another ill deed, a stain which, by the will of God, he may wash away with the tears of penitence, lest one excess counterbalance so great a sum of good actions. He raised the dam of the fishpond at Babwell, near the new mill, to such a height that owing to the holding back of the waters there was no man, rich or poor, who had land near the water from the gate of the town to the eastern gate,

who did not lose his garden and orchards. The pasture
of the cellarer, on one part of the bank, was lost, and
the arable land of the persons near was made worse.
The meadow of the cellarer, and the orchard of the
farmer, were swallowed up in the abundance of water,
and all the neighbours complained of the thing. And
when the cellarer complained to him in full chapter
about so great a loss, he at once answered with anger
that his fishpond should not suffer for the benefit of
our meadow.

WHETHER IT IS BETTER TO HAVE AN ABBOT FROM ONE'S OWN HOUSE

THE dean of London writes as follows in his
chronicles :—" King Henry the Second, having a discussion as to the vacant abbacies with the archbishop
and bishops, so observed the rule of the canons in the
matter of appointing abbots, as to make use of votes
obtained from other houses. Perhaps he thought that
if pastors were everywhere created by their own body,
the familiarity which had been contracted before election would lead to impunity for vices ; equality glosses
over faults ; and there will be too much slackness in
the cloisters."

Another has said, "It does not seem right that a pastor should be chosen from his own house, but rather from another. For if he be taken from another house, he will ever believe, according to size of the monastery which he has undertaken to rule, that many are wise, and will seek their counsel, if he be a good man, and if he be an evil man, he will fear their virtue. But a member of the house knows fully the ignorance, weakness and incompetence of all, and he will raven with the greater security, mingling square with round." The monks of Ramsey, acting on these grounds, when they had full power to choose whomsoever they would of their own number, twice elected an abbot from foreign houses, in our own times.

HOW THERE WAS A QUARREL WITH THE MONKS OF ELY

In the year of grace one thousand two hundred and one, the abbot of Flaix came to us, who with the

A.D. 1201.

assent of the abbot, and by his own preaching, caused public buyings and sellings which had taken place on Sundays in the market place to be abandoned, and it was decreed that they should be held on Mondays.

The same abbot did the like in many cities and boroughs of England.

And the same year, the monks of Ely set up a market for buying and selling at Lakenheath, for which they had the assent and charter of the king. But we, at first, with our friends and neighbours, labouring peacefully, sent messengers to the chapter of Ely, and also at first letters to the lord of Ely, praying that they would desist from that which had been begun. And we added that we would in a friendly manner pay the fifteen marks which had been given for the charter obtained from the king, for the sake of peace, and for the securing of the maintenance of mutual affection. What more need be said? They would not desist, and threatening words went to and fro, and spears threatened spears.

But we received a writ of recognition as to whether that market had been established to the prejudice of ourselves and to the injury of the market town of St. Edmund's. And oath was made, and it was protested that this was done to our injury. And when it was told to the king, the king caused inquest to be made by his registrar as to the kind of charter which he had given to the monks of Ely, and it was found that he

A.D. 1202.

had given them the said market under this condition, that it should not be to the detriment of the neighbouring markets.

However, the king, when forty marks were promised to him, made us a charter that no market should henceforth be made within the liberty of St. Edmund, without the assent of the abbot. And he wrote to Geoffrey FitzPeter, the justiciar, that the market of Lakenheath should be destroyed. Then the justiciar wrote to the sheriff of Suffolk to the same effect.

And the sheriff, knowing that he was not able to enter the liberties of St. Edmund, nor to exercise any power there, sent this to the abbot by his writ, that this same thing might be carried out according to the command of the king.

So the bailiff of the hundred came thither on the market day with the witness of the free men, and publicly forbade that market in the name of the king, and exhibited the letters of the king and of the sheriff. But being assailed with abuse and injuries, he departed without performing his work. But the abbot put off the matter for a time, and when he was in London, consulted the wise men on the point. Then he sent word to his bailiffs that they should take the men of St. Edmund, with horses and arms, and destroy the market, and if they found any buying or selling, they should bring them in bonds with them.

So at midnight, there went out almost six hundred men, well armed, making their way towards Laken-heath. But when the spies told that they were coming, all those who were in the market dispersed hither and thither, and not one was found. On the same night, however, the prior of Ely came with his officials, as he suspected the coming of our men, that he might defend so far as he could those who were selling and buying, but would not leave his lodging. And when our bailiffs demanded from him surety and pledge that he would stand his trial in the court of St. Edmund for the injury which he had done, and he would not give it, having taken counsel, they over-threw the shambles of the butchers and the stalls in the market, and carried them away with them; and they took with them all the cattle, sheep, and oxen, yea, and all the beasts of the field, and made their way towards Icklingham.

The bailiffs of the prior followed them, and asked for their cattle in pledge for fifteen days; and it was done as they asked. And within fifteen days there came a writ, in which the abbot was summoned to come to the exchequer to make answer for such a deed, and to the effect that the cattle which had been taken should in the meanwhile be sent back free. For the bishop of Ely, a man eloquent and cunning, had in person made complaint on this matter to the justiciar and to the magnates of England, saying that an unheard-of act of daring had been done in the land of St. Etheldreda in time of peace, whence also many were moved against the abbot.

HOW THE ABBOT DISPUTED WITH THE BISHOP OF ELY

MEANWHILE also other causes of dispute arose between the bishop of Ely and the abbot. For when a youth of Glemesford was accused in the court of St. Edmund for a breach of the king's peace, and had long been sought, and in this county, at last the bishop's seneschal produced that youth, and sought the court of St. Etheldreda for him, showing the charters and liberties of his lord. But our bailiffs, when they claimed the right to try the case and the possession of such liberty, could not be heard. For the county court placed the matter in respite until it might be decided before the itinerant justices, so that St. Edmund was driven from his jurisdiction.

HOW KING JOHN SUMMONED THE ABBOT TO HIM, AND OF THAT WHICH WAS DONE THEREUPON

Now when the abbot heard of this he proposed to cross the sea, but as he was ill, he wished to put it off until the feast of the Purification. And lo! on St. Agnes' day, there come a messenger from the king, bearing a brief from the lord pope, in which it was laid down that the lord of Ely and the abbot of St. Edmund's should make inquest concerning Geoffrey FitzPeter and William de Stuteville and certain other magnates of England, who had taken the cross, and for whose absolution the lord king made request, alleging the infirmity of their health, and the need of their advice for the preservation of his realm. And the same messenger bore letters of the lord king, ordering that when the letters had been read, the abbot should come to speak with him concerning the message of the lord pope.

A.D. 1203.
21ST JANUARY.

Then the abbot was disturbed, and said, "I am straitened on every side. I must offend either God or the king. By the true God, come what may, I will not knowingly lie." And so he came home with all speed, being rather weak with illness of body and mind, and being humbled and timid, contrary to his usual manner, by means of the prior, he sought counsel of us, which he had very rarely done hitherto. And he asked what was to be done about the threatened liberties of the church, and whence the expenses might be provided if he were to undertake this journey, and to whom the custody of the abbey should be given, and what was to be done as to the poor servants who had long time served him.

And it was answered that he should go in person, and that he should borrow enough money, which should be paid from our sacristy and pittances, and from our other revenues according to his will. And it was answered that he should commit the abbey to the care of the prior and of another clerk, whom he had enriched, and who could meanwhile live of his own, that thus the abbot might save expense, and that he should give money to his servants according to the time which they had served him. And when he had heard such counsel, he was pleased, and so it was done.

So the abbot came into the chapter next day, before his departure, and caused to be borne with him all his books, and he presented them to the church and monastery, and commended our counsel, which we had shown to him through the prior.

HOW THE ABBOT LEFT THE MONASTERY IN PEACE WITH ALL MEN

MEANWHILE we heard some murmuring and saying that the abbot was careful and thoughtful for his barony, but as to the liberties of the monastery, which we had lost in his time, that is, for the loss of the court and liberties of the cellarer, and for the liberties of the sacristan in the matter of the appointment of the bailiffs of the town by the monastery, he said nothing. Therefore the Lord stirred up the spirit of three brothers of moderate intelligence, and they, having roused many others, came to consult the prior on this matter, that on his departure the abbot might provide for the indemnity of his church in respect of her liberties.

When the abbot heard this, he answered many things which must not be spoken, swearing that he would be lord while he lived. But when vespers came, he spoke gently on the matter with the prior. And on the morrow, as he was about to depart and came to seek leave, as he sat in the chapter, he said that he had satisfied all his servants, and had made his will, as if he were then about to die. Then beginning to speak concerning the liberties of the church, he excused himself, saying that he had changed the ancient customs lest there might be a defect in the king's justice. And he cast the blame on the sacristan, and said that if Durand the bailiff, who was then ill, should die, the sacristan should hold the balliwick in his own hand, and should appoint a bailiff in the presence of the chapter, as had been the ancient custom, provided that this were done by the counsel of the abbot. But he would in no wise return the gifts and presents annually made by the bailiff.

And when we asked what was to be done in the matter of the court of the cellarer which had been lost, and especially as to the pence which the cellarer had been wont to receive for the renewal of pledges, he grew angry at this, and asked by what authority we exacted the right of royal justice, and those things which pertain to the royal powers. And the answer was that we had always had this from the foundation of the church and even for three years after he received the abbacy, and that we had this liberty still in all our manors for the renewal of pledges. And we said that we ought not to lose our right for the hundred shillings which he privately received each year from the bailiff, and we boldly demanded that we should have such seisin as we had in his day.

But the abbot, as he was in a strait how to answer, wishing to leave us in peace and to go away quietly, ordered that those pence, and the other things which the cellarer demanded, should be sequestrated until he should return.   And he promised that on his return he would in all things act with our advice, and would dispose things justly, and render to every man that which was his due.   With these words tranquillity was restored, but not for long, since, "Any man may be rich in promises."

NOTES

Page xxv. *The year in which the Flemings were taken.*—
The allusion is to the battle of Fornham, November, 1173. In
this year the quarrel between Henry II. and his sons, culminated
in a general rising both in Normandy and in England. Of the
leaders of the rebellion in England, Robert de Bellemont, earl
of Leicester, was the chief. Having gathered a force of mercenaries in the Low Countries, he landed at Walton, which he
failed to take. After joining hands with Hugh Bigod, earl of
Norfolk, at Framlingham, and capturing Haughley, he attempted
to force his way to his own estates. Meanwhile, the justiciar
Richard de Lucy and Humphrey Bohun hastened south from
their campaign against the Scots, and having been reinforced by
the local levies, they succeeded in intercepting Leicester at
Fornham St. Geneveve, on the river Lark, four miles north of
Bury St. Edmund's. The rebels were easily defeated, and
Leicester taken prisoner; of his mercenaries only a few escaped.
An account of the battle, not very accurate, from the point of
view of the St. Edmund's monks, is to be found in Appendix E
of the first volume of the *Memorials of St. Edmund's Abbey*
(Rolls Series). The escape of those mercenaries who did escape
is attributed to the intervention of St. Edmund and St. Thomas.

Page 1. *Abbot Hugh.*—Hugh, prior of Westminister, was
elected abbot in 1157, in succession to Abbot Ording. According to Gervase (I., 163) he received his benediction from

Theobald, archbishop of Canterbury, to whom he made profession of canonical obedience. According to the *Chronica Buriensis* (*Mem.* III., 6) he was confirmed by the bishop of Winchester. In any case, abbot Hugh, as is related in the text of the *Chronicle of Jocelin* (p. 6), was freed from all obedience by Pope Alexander III.

Page 1. *His eyes were dim.*—Gen. xxvii., 1.

Page 2. *Silken caps . . . were often placed in pledge.*—This was illegal. Rokewode (*Chron. Joc.*, pp. 106-7) gives instances of fines inflicted on Jews for taking church property in pawn, from the Pipe Rolls of Norfolk and Suffolk.

Ibid. The sacristan William.—William Wardell (*Mem.* II., 291). His incompetence is mentioned in the *Gesta Sacristarum* (*ibid.*), and is described in the text.

Page 3. *Letters of the lord king.*—The Jews were legally the king's chattels, and debts due to them were due to the king. Accordingly, when debtors failed to pay, the Jews were able to invoke the royal authority to enforce payment.

Page 6. *I was imprisoned.*—Arnold (*Mem.* I.. xliv., note 3 ; 212), gives reasons for supposing that this alludes to a second imprisonment of Samson, distinct from that which he suffered on his return from Rome (see text, p. 77). The passage would appear to refer to a recent event, which the imprisonment after his Roman journey was not.

Ibid. Sent to Acre.—In all probability this means Castle Acre, where was a famous Cluniac priory, founded by William de Warenne, as a cell to St. Pancras, Lewes. Acre, however. might mean either Castle Acre or West Acre, at both of which places were priories.

Page 6. *Their might is increased.*—Ps. cxxxiii., 6 (Vulgate).

Ibid. The Lord see and judge.—Ex. v., 21.

Ibid. Richard, archbishop of Canterbury.—Richard of Dover, Norman, prior of Dover, was archbishop from 1173 to 1184. He was elected at the end of the three years vacancy which followed on the murder of Beckett (Gervase, I., 244).

As to the question of the legatine authority over the abbey, Rokewood (p. 107-8) collects details. He points out that abbot Hugh appears to have obtained first a special exemption from Alexander III. from all authority other than that of the pope or a legate *a latere*; and afterwards a further exemption from the authority of archbishop Richard.

Page 9. *Pittance-master.*—The official of the monastery who had charge of the distribution of the pittances to the monks, that is, additional allowances of food or drink, the result of some benefaction.

Page 10. *Death of abbot Hugh.*—There is an account of this event in the *Chronica Buriensis* (*Mem*. III., 6).

Page 11. *Ranulf Glanvill.*—Justiciar from 1180 to 1189. He was deprived at the accession of Richard, and died on the crusade at the siege of Acre (1190), whither he had preceded Richard I. The news of the vacancy was sent to the justiciar, owing to the absence of Henry II. in Maine.

Page 12. *The wardship of the abbey.*—Rokewode (pp. 109-11) gives the accounts of the wardship from the Pipe Roll of Norfolk and Suffolk.

Ibid. How the prior ruled the Monastery.—The prior was Robert, who was appointed on the deposition of prior Hugh

(1173). He held office until his death, which took place about 1200 (see text, p. 194).

Page 13. *Blinded the eyes of all with gifts.*—Deut. xvi., 19.

Page 14. *Great tower of the church.*—The tower in the centre of the west front. It was begun probably either by abbot Baldwin (1065-97), or by abbot Robert I. (1100-02). It was blown down in 1210, before the death of Samson (*Ann. St. Edmund, Mem.* II., 18).

Page 16. *Thus was Samson mocked.*—Jud. xvi., 17.

Ibid. The two middle pillars.—Jud. xvi., 29.

Ibid. Well done good and faithful servant, etc.—Matt. xxv., 21.

Page 17. *Abbot Ording.*—Ording de Stowe was elected in 1183, when abbot Anselm was elected to the bishopric of London. Anselm was driven from his see soon afterwards on the ground that the election had taken place without the assent of the dean of London, and resumed his abbacy. On his death in 1148, Ording was again elected, and held the abbacy to his death in 1156. (*Chron. Bur., Mem.* III., 5-6.)

Ibid. Knowledge of binding and loosing.—Cp. Matt. xvi., 19.

Page 18. *Cheats of Norfolk.*—The allusion is to Samson, who was a native of Norfolk.

Ibid. Much learning has not made him mad.—Cp. Acts xxvi., 24.

Page 20. *Understood as a child,* etc.—I. Cor. xiii., 11.

Ibid. Fully persuaded in his own mind.—Rom. xiv., 5.

Page 21. *Season of blood letting.*—The monks practised blood-letting five times a year,—in September, before Advent and Lent, and after Easter and Pentecost, under the rule of St. Victor. An account of the manner in which it was practised at St. Edmund's is to be found in the *Liber Albus*. (Rokewode, p. 113, *Mem.* I. 221, note.)

Page 22.   *He that is able to receive it*, etc.—Matt. xiv., 12.

Ibid.   Augustine, archbishop of Norway.—Eystein, archbishop of Trondheim, was banished from Norway for political reasons and came to England in 1180. Rokewode (p. 113) collects from the accounts of the wardship of the abbey that he received £94 10s.

Page 23.   *Martyrdom of Saint Robert.*—Bale states that there was an account of the martyrdom of this child by the Jews, written by Jocelin.   The work, however, is not known to exist at the present day.   Gervase (I., 296) relates the event in somewhat similar terms to those in the text : "In this year, at Eastertide, a certain boy, Robert by name, was martyred by the Jews at St. Edmund's, and he was afterwards honourably buried in the church of St. Edmund, and became famous, as common report goes, for many miracles."   There is an account also in *Chron. Bur.* (*Mem.* III., 6) where the date (June 10th) is given.

Ibid.   Many signs and wonders, etc.—Acts v., 12.

Page 25.   *A perpetual shame.*—Jer. xxiii., 40.

Ibid.   Speaking by the spirit of God.—I. Cor xii., 3.

Page 26.   "*Verba mea.*"—Ps. v., Vulgate.

Page 27.   *His journey to Rome*—For Samson's own account of this, see text, p. 77ff.

Ibid.   Richard, Bishop of Winchester.—Richard Toclive, archdeacon of Poitiers (1162-73), elected bishop of Winchester in 1173; died in 1188.

Page 32. *Geoffrey the chancellor.*—Son of Henry II. by some woman of low birth. He became bishop-elect of Lincoln in 1173, but resigned his see and was made chancellor in 1182. In 1189 he secured the archbishopric of York by forgery, as his enemies asserted, and certainly by bribery. From that time his life was one long quarrel with Richard I. and John, and with the chapter of York and Hubert Walter, both as dean of York and as archbishop. Eventually, he fled into exile as the result of his refusal to meet the financial demands of John, and died in Normandy in 1212.

Ibid. The last first, etc.—Matt. xix., 30.

Page 33. *Nicholas de Waringford.*—A monk of St. Alban's, prior of Wallingford. He became abbot of Malmesbury about 1163, but was deposed in 1187. (Rokewode, p. 114.)

Page 34. *Lord H. de St. Neots.*—There was a Herbert, prior of St. Neot's in 1159 and in 1173. (Rokewood, p. 114.)

Page 36. *"Miserere mei, Deus."*—Ps. l, Vulgate.

Page 37. *The elect received his benediction.*—At Merewell, near Newport, I.W. He received his benediction from Richard of Winchester and Augustine, bishop of Waterford, on February 28th (*Chron., Bur., Mem.* III., 7, and *Ann. St. Ed., Mem.* II., 5). From the same sources we learn that Samson was received at St. Edmund's on Palm Sunday, March 21st.

Page 38. *"Benedictus Dominus."*—Response at matins after the second lesson on Trinity Sunday. (Rokewode, p. 18.)

Ibid. "Martiri adhuc."—A response following the sixth lesson at matins on St. Edmund's day. Rokewode (p. 115) gives the musical notes which accompany it from a life of the saint of the time of abbot Anselm. Rokewode seems to suggest that this was one of the antiphons composed in honour of St. Edmund by Warner, abbot of Rebaix, for which see Hermannus, *De Mir. St. Eadmundi* (*Mem.* I., 69-70).

Page 39. "*Omnipotens sempiterne Deus.*"—Liturgia Romana Vetus. (Rokewode p. 18, note 4.)

Ibid. *Wimer the sheriff.*—Rokewode (p. 116) collects from the Pipe Rolls of Norfolk and Suffolk that Wimer was sheriff of Norfolk and Suffolk in conjunction with Bartholomew Glanvill, and William Bardolf from the 16th to the 22nd years of Henry II.; and sheriff alone from then to the 34th year of Henry II.

Page 40. *New Seal.*—A reproduction of this seal appears as a frontispiece to Rokewode's edition.

Ibid. *Ordered his household.*—John vi., 6.

Page 42. *Henry his nephew.*—Rokewode (p. 116ff) prints the charters upon which Henry de Hastings claimed to be hereditary steward of the liberty of St. Edmund's.

Page 43. *Injury for injury.*—For the way in which this threat was carried out, see text, p. 104.

Page 45. *His Calendar.*—Rokewode (p. 121) mentions a transcript of the Calendar which was in a copy of the *Liber de Consuetudinibus S. Edmundi* in his possession.

Page 49. *Arise up quickly.*—Acts xxii., 7.

Page 54. *Believe every spirit.*—I. John iv., 1.

Ibid. *Judgment rejoiceth against mercy.*—Cp. James ii., 13.

Page 56. *Those of Melun.*—Peter Abelard founded a school of dialectic at Melun.

Page 62. *Had been a monk for seventeen years.*—The *Ann. St. Ed.* (*Mem.* II., 5) bear this out, as under 1166 there is an entry. "Abbot Samson was made a monk." (Cp. *Mem.* I., xliv.)

Page 63. *Fall of Jerusalem.*—Jerusalem was taken by Saladin on October 2nd, 1187.

Page 70. *By the sale of holy water.*—It was the common practice to devote the money derived from the sale of holy water to the support of poor clerks. The synod of Exeter (1287) definitely provided that such profits should be so spent. (*Mem.* I., 247, note *b.*)

Ibid. Fitz-Elias.—As to grants of land to Elias, by abbot Hugh, see Rokewode (p. 122). The total amounted to one hundred and forty acres, of which sixty were in Elmswell.

Page 71. *William, son of William of Diss.*—This is the compiler of the passage dealing with the claims of the Cokefield family which appears at the end of Jocelin's *Chronicle* (see note to p. 153).

Page 72. *Appointed them for the maintenance of the schools.*— The date of the foundation of the school by abbot Samson is uncertain. But as there is a grant to the master in 1198, the foundation was probably made early in the abbacy of Samson. (Cp. Rokewode, p. 123).

Page 73. *The expulsion of the Jews.*—Arnold (*Mem.* I., 249, note) points out that, in the absence of any royal castle to which the Jews might retire for safety, their expulsion was really in their own interests. They would otherwise be always liable to massacre, and especially at this particular time, which was marked by an outburst of fanaticism against the Jews, who were massacred in many towns, especially at York. Diceto (II., 75-6) mentions the massacre of fifty-seven Jews at St. Edmund's on Palm Sunday, 1190.

NOTES

Page 74. *Mildenhall.*—This manor was in the hands of the Crown in Domesday. It had, however, been granted to St. Edmund by the charter of Edward the Confessor, and was held by a certain Stigand during the life of Edward (*Mem.* I., 48 and 250, note *a*; cp. *Monasticon* III., 188). The present transaction is related by Benedictus (II., 91; cp. Hoveden, III., 18) "And Samson, abbot of St. Edmund's, bought from king Richard the manor, which is called Mildenhall, for one thousand marks, because it was said to have belonged originally to the abbey of St. Edmund's."

Ibid. Great Roll of Winchester.—That is, Domesday Book.

Ibid. Queen Eleanor . . . had the right to receive a hundred marks.—This was the "aurum reginæ" or queen-gold, a due of ten per cent., to be paid by everyone who made a gift to the king. (Blackstone, quoted by Arnold, *Mem.* I., 250, note *c*.)

Page 75. *Ransom of king Richard.*—Richard was ransomed from Henry VI., for 100,000 marks of silver "according to the standard of Koln," (Hoveden, III., 215-6. Diceto, II., 110.) The demands made on the clergy and laity may be found in Hoveden (III., 208 ff). All the monasteries were obliged to hand over their gold and silver, which was placed in the hands of royal commissioners appointed to superintend the raising of the ransom. (Hoveden, III., 210.)

Ibid. The queen redeemed the same chalice.—The charter of release is printed in Dugdale's *Monasticon* (Ed. 1846; Vol. III., 154).

Page 76. *Hospital at Babwell.*—Traces of this are to be found in a small ruin near the railway bridge on the Thetford road. (Arnold, *Mem.* I., 252, note *a*.)

Page 76. *A charter from the king.*—On this charter, see Rokewode (p. 124-5).

Ibid. Walter of Coutances.—Elected bishop of Lincoln and consecrated in 1183. In the next year he was translated to Rouen. He was one of Richard I.'s most trusted servants, and was sent to England to settle the disputes which arose between Longchamp and John after the departure of Richard on the crusade. He died in 1207.

Page 77. *The schism between Alexander and Octavian.*—On the death of Adrian IV., in 1159, Cardinal Roland was elected by a majority only, and took the name of Alexander III. The imperialist party, however, declared Cardinal Octavian pope under the name of Victor IV. Octavian was supported by the citizens of Rome and by the emperor, and recognised by the imperial synod of Pavia. Alexander took refuge in France. Victor died (1164) without the dispute having been finally settled. (Cp. Gregorovius, *City of Rome in the Middle Ages* (Eng. trans.) Vol. IV., p. 563ff.)

Ibid. I, however, pretended that I was a Scot.—Arnold (*Mem*, I., xliii.) gives as the reason for Samson's action the fact that Scotland favoured the party of Octavian, in opposition to the English support of Alexander.

Ibid. Ride, ride, Rome, etc.—Arnold (*Ibid.*, note 1) gives as the meaning of this, "I am riding towards Rome, turning from Canterbury." He adds, "If he had meant to say, 'returning from Canterbury,' he would at once have been taken for an English adherent of Alexander."

Page 78. *Geoffrey Ridel.*—Archdeacon of Canterbury, and a strenuous opponent of Becket. He was elected to Ely in 1173, and died in 1189. In the text of the *Chronicle* there will be found an account of a dispute between him and Samson, as to the bishop's right to demand timber (p. 113ff.).

Page 79. *Exiled to Acre.*—As to this, see note to p. 6.

Page 80. *Archbishop Baldwin.*—Bishop of Worcester (1180-83). He was elected to Canterbury, after some dispute, on the death of Richard of Dover, December, 1183. (Gervase, I., 311 ff.) Died, 1190, at the siege of Acre.

Page 81. *At the beginning of the fasting time.*—Gervase (I., 353) mentions the meeting and supplies the date.

Page 82. *Which will allow this.*—That is, will admit that the abbey has possessed this jurisdiction from time immemorial. (*Mem* I., 256, note.)

Ibid. He that is able to receive it, etc.—Matt. xix., 12.

Page 83. *Lord bishop of Ely.*—William Longchamp, elected to Ely and made justiciar and joint regent at the accession of Richard I. He was driven from office in 1191, owing to the opposition of John and Hugh Puiset, bishop of Durham. He died in 1197.

Ibid. Scenting the archbishopric.—The archbishopric remained vacant from the death of Baldwin until 1191—over a year—when Reginald, bishop of Bath, was elected. He died less than fifteen days later. (Benedictus, II., 226-7.) The archbishopric then remained vacant again until the election of Hubert Walter, 1193.

Ibid. The chancellor did not condescend to make any answer.—The pride of Longchamp is the common theme of all the chroniclers, who unite in attributing his fall to this fault.

Having obtained the legation from Clement III., he claimed to
be supreme over church and state alike, refusing (perhaps in
accord with Richard's instructions) to admit that he had any
colleague in the office of justiciar. His character is sketched in
a letter of Hugh Nunant, bishop of Coventry, which is to be
found in Benedictus (II., 215-20.) "He was a man great among
all the people of the west, as one having power over the kingdom
and the authority of the apostolic see, being as it were ambidex-
trous. . . . He seemed, indeed, to divide the elements with
God, leaving heaven alone to the God of heaven. . . . From sea
to sea he was feared as God, and were I to say more than God,
I should not lie, for God is long-suffering and merciful, but he
did all things ill and in haste." William of Newburgh calls him
"that rhinocerous." Richard of Devizes calls him "that three-
named and threefold man."

   Page 84. *When the same chancellor had returned from Germany.*
—Longchamp, after failing to persuade the regency to permit his
return before, came back to England in 1193, with letters from
Henry VI. as to the ransom of Richard. (Hoveden, III., 211.)

   Ibid. The violence done to the archbishop of York.—Richard
had forbidden Geoffrey to visit England for three years, but the
archbishop landed at Dover. There he was arrested by order of
Longchamp, but released on the intervention of John. (Benedictus, II., 106; 209-11.) As to the excommunication of
Longchamp, this is mentioned by Benedictus (II., 211-12), and
by Richard of Devizes (pp. 36, 43, 56). Ralph de Diceto
(II., 98) makes the excommunication general only.

   Page 85. *When king Henry had taken the Cross.*—At Gisors,
1188.

Page 85. *John, bishop of Norwich.*—John of Oxford, elected to Norwich in 1175; died, 1200. As a matter of fact, John did not go to Palestine. He was waylaid and robbed on his journey, and obtained absolution from his vow from the pope. Richard made this excuse for levying a heavy fine. (Hoveden, III., 42. Richard of Devizes, p. 12.)

Ibid. Capture of king Richard.—Richard was captured in December, 1192, near Vienna, and imprisoned at Durrenstein. In the following year he was handed over to the emperor Henry VI. and imprisoned in various castles in Germany. Hoveden (III., 198) only mentions the abbots of Boxley and Robertsbridge as going to search for Richard, and it would seem that Samson merely offered to go, though it appears that he did subsequently visit Germany (see text, p. 87).

Page 86. *Council of London.*—The council is mentioned by Benedictus (II., 106). Richard of Devizes (p. 14) mentions that at this council Longchamp gave judgment that the monks should be expelled from Coventry, in accordance with the wishes of Hugh Nunant.

Page 87. *Siege of Windsor.*—John, acting in concert with Philip Augustus, availed himself of the opportunity afforded by Richard's capture to stir up disorder in England. He captured Windsor, and demanded the fealty of the kingdom from the justiciars. On their refusal, he fortified his castles against them. The justiciars, however, under the direction of Hubert Walter, acted promptly, and soon compelled the surrender of all John's castles, except Nottingham and Tickhill. Windsor was handed over to the custody of Eleanor. (Hoveden, III., 204-7.)

Ibid. Leave was granted to knights to hold tournaments.—The object of this provision is explained by Diceto (II., 120-1), and was to raise money for the king by the sale of licences. The rates at which the licences were sold were twenty silver marks for an earl, ten for a baron, three for a knight holding land, and two for a knight not holding land. (Hoveden, III., 268.)

Page 88. *Archbishop Hubert.*—Hubert Walker, dean of York (1188), and bishop of Salisbury (1189). He went on the crusade, and was present at the siege of Acre. He was elected archbishop in 1193, and died in 1205.

Page 90. *Earl de Clare.*—Richard de Clare, fourth earl of Hertford (d. 1218), one of the twenty-five barons appointed to enforce the observance of Magna Carta.

Ibid. Earl Alberic.—Alberic de Vere, first earl of Oxford (d. 1194). For his subsequent quarrel with Samson, see text, p. 106.

Ibid. Alfric, son of Withgar.—For details as to his holding, see Rokewode, p. 129.

Page 91. *Earl Roger Bigod.*—Second earl of Norfolk, died 1221. One of the twenty-five barons of Magna Carta.

Ibid. The standard of St. Edmund.—Rokewode (pp. 122-31) quotes a passage from Lydgate's metrical life of St. Edmund on the subject. The whole poem was printed by C. Horstmann in his *Altenglische Legenden*, Heilbron, 1881. (See *Mem.* III., l.-li.) A reproduction of the standard is published as a tailpiece to Rokewode's edition.

Ibid. Thomas de Mendham.—He held a knight's fee in Livermere. (See Rokewode, p. 132, who appends other details.) He was possibly descended from a brother of abbot Baldwin, and seems to have been constable to the monastery.

Page 93. *Eight hundreds and a half.*—The grant of this land which had been held by Emma of Normandy, wife of Ethelred II., was granted to St. Edmund by Edward the Confessor on the occasion of his visit to the monastery in 1044. (*Mem.*, I., 363, cp. Rokewode, pp. 132-33, and Hermannus, in *Mem.*, I., 48.) The hundreds were Thingoe, Thedwastre, Blackburne, Bradborn, Bradmere, Risbridge, Babery, and half that of Exning. (*Mem.*, I., xxviii., note 1.) The charter is printed in Dugdale's *Monasticon* (III., 138, No. vii., ed. 1846).

Page 93. *The abbot confirmed to him all his other lands.*—The lands confirmed to him were those which he held in Lafham, Whetfeld, Wordsey, Navelton, Lilesey, and Bretenham. (Rokewode, p. 132.)

Page 94. *Herbert the dean.*—He received a grant of lands from abbot Ording, his cousin. (Rokewode, p. 133.)

Ibid. Haberdon.—"Within the bounds of St. Edmundsbury, lies behind Southgate street, extending to the river Lark, contiguous to the parish of Rougham." (Rokewode, p. 133.)

Page 96. *The churches of Westley*, etc.—Rokewode (p. 133-4) collects the evidence of the possession of these churches by St. Edmund.

Ibid. Darrein presentment.—An inquest for the purpose of discovering the person who last presented to a benefice.

Page 97. *William, bishop of Norwich.*—William de Turbeville, bishop of Norwich, 1146 to 1174. He was a strong adherent of Becket.

Page 102. *Staffacres and foracres.*—"These staffacres, it would seem, were certain payments or fees due to the abbot's staff or crozier." (Rokewode, p. 134.) Arnold (*Mem.* I., 268, note) suggests that the foracres were similar payments for the right of attending the market (*forum*).

Page 104. *Abbot Samson began a struggle with his knights.*—Rokewode (p. 134-5) gives a list of the knights in 3 *Ric.* I. As to the struggle, compare the text, p. 43.

Page 108. *Concerning Henry of Essex.*—This passage, as would appear from the terms of the first paragraph, is an interpolation by some other writer than Jocelin. Gervase (i., 165) mentions the conduct of Henry of Essex on the Welsh expedition, and the disastrous result of the English army. He adds, "Owing to this accident, Henry, who had been the noblest among the princes of England, suffered everlasting shame and disinheritance." Diceto (I., 310) mentions the duel. (Cp. *Mem.* I., 272, note.)

Page 110. *Roger, earl of Clare.*—In the Latin there is here a play upon words : "comes Clarensis, clarus," etc., which cannot be rendered in a translation.

Page 115. *Forty pounds ought to be rendered from the town.*—Rokewode (p. 136) states that Eugenius III. confirmed the appropriation of the rents of the town to the use of the sacrist, in the days of abbot Ording.

Page 117. *Moot-horn.* The horn which was sounded to summon to assemblies of the moots or meetings, whether of the shire or boroughs. (Cp. Rokewode, p. 136-7.)

Page 119. *Tol and theam.*—These two words are defined in Stubb's *Select Charters* (glossary) as follows : "Tol, duty on imports. Theam, the right of compelling the person in whose hands stolen or lost property was found to vouch to warranty, that is, to name the person from whom he received it." On the other hand, the terms, in conjunction with infangenthef, are often used as a mere jingle which has no particular meaning; and taken together, tol and theam may be said to mean the ordinary rights conferred on towns—that is, a vague concession.

Page 120. *The Philistines be upon thee, Samson.*—Jud. xvi., 9.

Page 124. *This also the abbot graciously granted.*—Samson's charter is to be found in the *Monasticon* (Rokewode, p. 137).

Page 126. *How is the gold become dim,* etc.—Lament. iv., 1.

Page 128. *Abbot Robert.*—Robert II. (1107-12). The charter of Henry I. confirming this division is to be found in the *Monasticon* (ed. 1846, III., 152, No. xiv).

Ibid. Introduced innovations by his legatine authority.—Hubert Walter received the legation from Celestine III. in 1195. An account of his proceedings on the visitation of York, and the decrees which he issued there, are to be found in Hoveden (III., 293-7). Hoveden (III., 299) also relates the deposition of the abbot of Thorney by Hubert Walter at this time.

Page 129. *Dereham.*—West Dereham, in Norfolk, was the birthplace of Hubert Walter.

Page 131. *The lord pope wrote.*—Innocent III., who became pope in 1198, confirmed the privileges of St. Edmund, especially those granted by Alexander and Urban (Rokewode, p. 137). Arnold (*Mem.* I., 285, note) suggests that as no such letter as that described in the text can be found, Jocelin misunderstood the statement of Samson, and that he really refers to the letter addressed by Innocent to the abbot and convent of St. Edmund.

Page 133. *That the lord of York was coming to England as Legate.*—After having tried in vain to obtain a decision in his favour from Celestine III., Geoffrey secured such a decision from

Innocent (Hoveden, IV., 67). The report that he was to receive legatine authority was, however, unfounded.

Page 134. *King Richard sent orders to all the bishops and abbots of England that every nine knights should furnish a tenth.*—Hoveden (IV., 40), appears to relate the same demand as is here mentioned by Jocelin. "In this year [1198] Richard asked, through Hubert Walter, that the men of the kingdom of England should find him three hundred knights or give him so much money as would enable him to hire three hundred knights to serve for one year, at the rate of three Angevin shillings for each knight per diem." All the rest assented to the demand, but Hugh of Avalon, bishop of Lincoln, refused to do so.

Page 135. *Castle of Eu.*—This castle was restored to Richard by the treaty of Issoudun (1196). The terms of the truce are to be found in Hoveden (IV., 3).

Page 141. *A scorn and derision to those who were round about us.*—Ps. xliv., 13.

Page 142. *The anniversary of abbot Robert.*—Robert II. died on 16th September, 1112 (*Chron. Bur. Mem.*, III., 5). His festival, however, was kept on September 28th (Arnold, *Mem.*, I., 291, note). Rokewode (p. 139), quoting the *Liber Albus*, gives September 16th as his day, and for those of Ording and Hugh, January 30th and November 14th respectively.

Page 145. *Meetings and sports and matches.*—Rokewode (p 139) says that these shows were probably miracle-plays, and notes from the text that Samson did occasionally entertain minstrels (cp. text, p. 67).

Page 147. *A commission of the lord pope.*—An account of this commission is to be found in Gervase (i., 550), while in Hove-

den (IV., 35-7), there is to be found the papal letter giving
orders for their restoration. As to their expulsion by Hugh
Nunant, see note to page 86. In Richard of Devizes there is an
amusing description of his hatred for monks (pp. 64-7).

Page 149. *He that has ears to hear*, etc.—Matt. xi., 15.

Page 151. *Hugh the sacristan.*—On the deposition of William
Wardell, abbot Samson appointed his namesake the precentor as
sacristan, as appeared from *Jocelin* (text, pp. 46 and 48). Appar-
ently the appointment was merely a temporary one. In the
Gesta Sacristarum (*Mem.* II., 291-2) Hugh is given as the successor
of William Wardell, and an account of his acts is to be found
there.

Page 153. *Adam de Cokefield died.*—For an exhaustive note
on the family of Cokefield, and for a genealogical table, see
Rokewode (pp. 140-8). At the end of the *Chronicle of Jocelin*
there is an appendix which deals with this family, and which was
written by William of Diss, the chaplain. It is here translated:
"Robert de Cokefield acknowledged to the lord abbot Samson,
in the presence of many, to wit, master W. de Banham, brother
W. de Diss, chaplains; William de Breiton, and many others,
that he ought to have no hereditary right in the townships of
Groton and Semere. Since, in the days of king Stephen, when
the peace was disturbed, the monks of St. Edmund, with the
assent of the abbot, had granted the said two townships to Adam
de Cokefield, his father, to be held by him all the days of his life,
namely: Semere for an annual rent of a hundred shillings, and
Groton on condition that he made an annual payment for it.
This was done because Adam was able to defend the said townships against the neighbouring owners of castles, that is, against

W. de Milding, and against W. de Ambley, because he had a
castle of his own near the said manors, that is, the castle of
Lilesey.　After the death of the said Adam, the said manors were
granted by the monks to Robert de Cokefield, son of the same
Adam, the rent of Semere being doubled, that is, ten pounds were
paid for it each year, so long as the lord abbot and the monastery
willed it; but he never had a charter on this matter, even for
the term of his life.　He had good charters for all the holdings
which he held from St. Edmund by hereditary rights, which I,
William, surnamed de Diss, who was then chaplain, read to the
audience of many, and in the presence of the said abbot; that is,
for the lands of Lilesey, which Ulfric de Lilesey held in the same
township of St. Edmund; and a charter of the abbot and monastery for the socages of Rougham, which the lady Rohesia de
Cokefield, wife of the former Adam the younger, had as her
dower; and for the lands which Lemer, his ancestor, had by
hereditary right in the township of Cokefield. which, in the days
of king Stephen, by assent of Anselm, abbot of St. Edmund's,
were converted into the fee of half a knight, whereas they had
formerly been socages of St. Edmund.　Moreover he had charters
of the abbot and monastery of St. Edmund for the lands which
were in the township of St. Edmund, namely, for the land of
Hemfrid Criketot, where the houses of the lady Adelaide were
formerly situated.　They have a charter and hereditary right,
for the payment of twelve pence, for the great messuage, where
the hall of the elder Adam de Cokefield had formerly been
situated with a wooden belfry, (?) one hundred and forty feet * in

---

* According to the Latin "two thousand."　Arnold conjec-
tures *septies* for *centies*, and this conjecture has been adopted
above.

height, for these they had a confirmation of their hereditary
right under a charter of the abbot and monastery, in which
charter the length and breadth of the said tower and messuage
were set forth, all of which was to be held at a payment of two
shillings. They have also a charter of hereditary right for the
lands which Robert de Cokefield, son of Odo de Cokefield, now
holds in Barton; but they have no charter for the township of
Cokefield, that is for the portion thereof which is devoted to
the support of the monks of St. Edmund. For that they have
one writ of King Henry the First, in which the king commands
abbot Anselm to allow Adam de Cokefield the elder to hold in
peace the firm of Cokefield and of other places, as long as he
pays the full firm; but that writ is sealed only in one place,
showing the effigy of the king, contrary to the manner adopted
in all royal writs. But Robert de Cokefield acknowledged in
the presence of the lord abbot and of the said witnesses, that he
believed that Cokefield was his by his hereditary right on the
ground of long tenure, since his grandfather Lemer held that
manor before the day of his death, and the elder Adam, his son,
for the term of his life, and Robert himself for all his life, in all
for some sixty years; but they never held a charter of the abbot
or monastery of St. Edmund in respect of the said land."

Page 155. *From the time when the town of St. Edmund's received the name and liberty of a borough.*—The liberties of St.
Edmund's originated from the abbots, and not from the crown,
and it would seem that they were first granted in the time of
Edward the Confessor. It was at this time also that the name
of St. Edmund's was substituted for that of Beodoricsworth.
The condition of the town in the time of *Domesday* may be
found in Rokewode, who translates the passage dealing with

St. Edmund's (p. 148-9), and in the appendix to the *Memorials* (I., 339). Some account of the progress made by St. Edmund's in the interval between *Domesday* and the time of abbot Samson is to be found in the Introduction by Arnold to the *Memorials* (Vol. I.)

Page 158. *Within the jurisdiction of the abbey.*—This amounted to the distance of one mile's radius by the charter of Edward the Confessor (*Mon.*, III., 138, No. vii., ed. 1846), and by a bull of Alexander III. (Rokewode, p. 149).

Ibid. Villeins adscript to the soil.—Lancetti. As to their duties, see Rokewode, p. 150.

Page 160. *The manor of Beodric.*—Beodricsworth means the "estate of Beodric." The name itself means "a table chieftain," according to Arnold (*Mem.*, I., iv., note). Abbo (*Mem.*, I., 19) calls the place "a royal township," which may be explained by the statement of Hermannus (*Mem.*, I., 33) that Beodric was of the royal house of East Anglia, and that the township was granted to him by a king of the same name.

Page 161. *To go to Lakenheath and bring back a catch of eels from Southrey.*—For the grant of fish by Elfgiva, wife of Canute, see *Monasticon* (ed. 1846, III., 137, No. v.). Cp. Rokewode (pp. 150-1).

Page 164. *In honour preferring one another.*—Rom. xii., 10.

Page 167. *In wrath remember mercy.*—Hab. iii., 2.

Page 169. *Nothing is hid which shall not be revealed.*—Luke xii., 2.

Page 170. *That the mouth of those who speak lies might be stopped.*—Ps. lxiii., 11.

Page 174. *Hear, O Heaven,* etc.—Isai. i., 2.

Page 175. *The holy body lay where is was wont to lie.*—That is, where it has lain since its translation by abbot Baldwin in 1095, for an account of which see Hermanus (*Mem.*, I., 84-9). The various translations of the relics of the saints are noticed in the table of dates to be found at the end of these notes.

Page 179. *Aylwin the monk.*—He was chief keeper of the shrine, in the days before the substitution of monks for secular clergy. On the news of the invasion of Sweyn (1010) he removed the relics to London, where they remained for three years. At a subsequent date he became a monk at the monastery of St. Edmund. An account of him is to be found in Hermannus (*Mem.*, I., 35-42), and in Samson's work, *De Miraculis Sancti Aedmundi* (*Mem.*, I., 116-132). Rokewode (pp. 153-4) quotes a passage on Aylwin from Lydgate's metrical life of the saint.

Page 181. *Shrine of St. Botolph.*—The relics of St. Botolph, "the kindly priest," were translated, together with other relics, at the time of the translation of the body of St. Edmund by abbot Baldwin in 1095. (Hermannus, *Mem.*, I., 88.) Nothing authentic is really known of him, but the supposed date of his death is 655.

Page 182. *King John . . . at once came to St. Edmund's.*— The visit of John to St. Edmund's is mentioned by Diceto (II., 166). Rokewode (p. 154) notes a second visit of John, when he acted with greater generosity, making an annual grant of ten marks. Even on this occasion, however, the gift was only in return for the giving back of a previous gift which he had made of a valuable ring, and which was to be returned to him for his life.

Page 184.   *I have nourished.*—etc.—Isai. i., **2.**

Page 185.   *Verba mea.*—Ps. v., i.

Ibid.   Every kingdom, etc.—Matt., xii., 25.

Page 187.   *The storm ceased,* etc.—Mark iv., 39.

Page 192.   *When Adam de Cokefield died.*—Cp. note to p. 153.

Page 194.   *I will not give my glory to another.*—Isai. xlvi., 8.

Ibid.   The abbot of Cluny.—An account of the visit of the abbot of Cluny is to be found in Diceto II., 173). The abbot was Hugh, who had been abbot of Reading. Rokewode (p. 155) mentions that this case was quoted to prove that the English Benedictine abbots owed no allegiance to Cluny.

Page 198.   *Between leprosy and leprosy.*—Deut. xvii., 8.

Page 202.   *Sharpened their tongues,* etc.—Ps. lxiii., 4, Vulgate.

Page 204.   *A little leaven leaveneth the whole lump.*—Gal. v., 9.

Page 205.   *The dean of London.*—Ralph de Diceto, who was for over fifty years archdeacon of Middlesex and dean of St. Paul's His name, de Diceto, presents considerable difficulty, and in the opinion of Stubbs (Introduction to the Rolls Series edition), it was an assumed name. Ralph died about 1203. The quotation in the text is from the *Imagines Historiarum* (I. 401-2; cp. note, p. 402), and deals with the conduct of Henry II. in the matter of filling up vacancies. Diceto says that the reason for Henry's conduct was a fear lest otherwise the royal power over elections and abbeys might be diminished.

Page 206.   *The abbot of Flaix.*—Hoveden (IV., 123-4) gives an account of the mission of Eustace, abbot of St. Germer de Flaix:—"In the same year (A.D. 1200) Eustace, abbot of Flaix, one of the followers of the said Fulk (de Neuilly) came to

England from Normandy to preach the word of the lord; and he performed miracles while he yet lived." Hoveden goes on to relate the blessing of a fountain at Wye, and the cure of a demoniac woman; the striking of a rock at Romney whence water came. He insisted on Sunday observance in London (cp. text), and urged the importance of almsgiving. But having roused much opposition in England "among the ministers of Satan," he soon returned to Normandy. Hoveden (IV., 167-9) gives a copy of the letter which Eustace alleged that he had received from heaven, and relates several other miracles (IV., 169-172). The results of his preaching were not permanent, and the practice of holding markets on Sundays was resumed (Hoveden, IV., 172).

Page 210. *Bishop of Ely.*—Eustace, dean of Salisbury, succeeded Longchamp as bishop of Ely (1197). Assisted Langton against John. Died 1215.

Page 211. *A brief from the lord pope.*—This brief is printed in Migne's *Patrologia* (214), among the letters of Innocent III. for 1202 (Arnold, *Mem.* I., 331 note).

Ibid. Letters of the lord king.—The summons of abbot Samson is noted in Diceto (II. 173). The bishops of Ely, Salisbury, and London, and the abbots of St. Edmund's, Westminster, and Tewkesbury were summoned to Normandy.

TABLE OF DATES

A.D.

870. November 30th. Edmund, king of the East Angles, defeated and slain by Inguar the Dane, at the battle of Hoxne.

870 ? The remains of Edmund placed in a tomb at Hoxne, the head being laid with the body. A chapel built over them.

903-41. Translation of the relics to Beodricsworth. (The date of the translation is variously given; cp. *Mem.*, I., xxi. It is, however, to be placed somewhere between 903, the year given by the "thirty-three years" of the Curteys Register, and 941, the date of the death of Athelstan, in whose reign Hermannus places the event.)

A wooden chapel is built over the shrine.

945. Edmund, son of Edward the Elder, grants the lands round Beodricsworth for the maintenance of the shrine. Four priests and two deacons are appointed as guardians of the shrine, the first six being, "Leofric the deacon, Leofric the priest, Alfrid, Bomfild, Kenelm, and Eilmund."

970 (*circa*). Abbo of Fleury writes the *Passio Sancti Eaamunai*, addressed to Dunstan as archbishop.

1010. Thurkill the Dane lands at Ipswich, and Aylwin, chief keeper of the shrine, removes the relics to London.

1013. The relics are brought back from London to Beodricsworth.

1020. The secular clergy, who had been keepers of the shrine,
are replaced by twenty Benedictine monks from St.
Benet Hulme and Ely. Uvius, prior of Hulme, first
abbot.

A stone church built over the shrine by order of Canute,
in reparation, it is alleged, for the wrongs done to
St. Edmund by his father Sweyn.

1028. Charter of Canute to the monastery of St. Edmund.

1032. Agelnoth, archbishop of Canterbury, consecrates the
new church.

1044. Visit of Edward the Confessor to the shrine.

Charter of Edward the Confessor.

About this time Beodricsworth becomes known as St.
Edmund's.

1050-60. Abbot Leofstan views the corpse of St. Edmund.

1071. Abbot Baldwin defeats the attempt of Erfast, bishop of
Thetford, to remove his episcopal seat to St. Edmund's,
by appealing to Alexander II., who issues a bull to
St. Edmund's.

1095. Translation of the relics by abbot Baldwin.

1095 (*circa*). Hermannus writes the *De Miraculis Sancti Eadmundi*.

1097. Abbot Baldwin builds a new church over the shrine.

1102. Abbot Robert I., son of Hugh Lupus, earl of Chester, is
deposed for simony by St. Anselm.

1135. Birth of Samson de Tottington.

1156. Hugh I., prior of Westminster, elected abbot.

1159-63. Journey of Samson to Rome on the matter of the
church of Woolpit.

First imprisonment of Samson at Castle Acre.

1166. Samson becomes a monk at St. Edmund's.

1172. Abbot Hugh obtains exemption from legatine authority.

1173. Battle of Fornham.

? Second banishment of Samson to Castle Acre.

Deposition of Prior Hugh; Robert made prior.

Jocelin de Brakelond becomes a monk at St. Edmund's.

1180. Journey of abbot Hugh to Canterbury. He falls from
his horse near Rochester (September 9th).

Abbot Hugh returns to the abbey.

(November 15th). Death of abbot Hugh.

1180-2. Vacancy in the abbacy. Robert the prior rules the
house, while Robert de Cokefield and Robert de Flamvill have the wardship of the abbot's lands.

Samson, subsacristan, conducts building and repairs.

1181 (June 10th). Martyrdom of St. Robert.

Residence of the archbishop of Norway in the abbey.

1182. The delegates of the monastery appear before Henry II.
to choose a new abbot.

Election of Samson as abbot (February 21st).

Samson received the benediction (February 28th).

Arrival of Samson at St. Edmund's (March 21st).

Samson made a judge in eccleiastical causes.

1198. Samson views the corpse of St. Edmund.

1210. Fall of abbot Samson's tower.

1212 (December 30th). Death of abbot Samson.

1539. Dissolution of the monastery of St. Edmund.

LIST OF THE ABBOTS OF ST. EDMUND'S

   i. Uvius, prior of St. Benet Hulme (1020).
  ii. Leofstan (1044).
 iii. Baldwin de St. Denis (1065).
  iv. Robert I. (1100).
   v. Robert II. (1102).
  vi. Albold (1114).
 vii. Anselm (1121 and 1138).
viii. Ording (1138 and 1148).
  ix. Hugh I. (1157).
   x. Samson de Tottington (1182).
  xi. Hugh II. (1215).
 xii. Richard de Lisle (1229).
xiii. Henry de Rushbrook (1234).
xiv. Edmund de Walpole (1248).
 xv. Simon de Luton (1257).
xvi. John de Norwold (1279).
xvii. Thomas de Tottington (1302).
xviii. Thomas de Draughton (1312).
xix. William de Bernham (1335).
 xx. Henry de Hunstanton (1361).
xxi. John de Brinkele (1361).

xxii. Edward Bromfield (1379).
xxiii. John de Tymworth (1385).
xxiv. William Cratfield (1390).
xxv. William Excetre (1415).
xxvi. William Curteys (1429).
xxvii. William Babyngton (1446).
xxviii. John Boon (1453).
xxix. Robert Ixworth (1469).
xxx. Richard Hengham (1474).
xxxi. Thomas Ratlisden (1479).
xxxii. William Codenham (1497).
xxxiii. William Bunting (1511).
xxxiv. John Melford (1514).

November 4th, 1539.—Dissolution of the monastery.

INDEX

Acre (Castle Acre), 6, 27, 79, 132

Adam, 204

Alberic, earl (de Vere), 90, 106, 187

Albinus, monk, 192

Alexander III., pope, 77

Alfric, son of Withgar, 90

Alpheton, 102

Alueth, Gilbert de, monk, 26

Ambrose, monk, 25

Ampton, 190

Andrew, monk, 25

Anselm, abbot, 124

Ansty, Hubert de, 189

Anthony, monk, 26

Arnald, 50, 51

Ashfield, 189, 190

Augustine, archbishop of Norway, 23; monk, 177

Aylwin, monk, 179

Babwell, 73, 76, 204, 205

Baldwin, archbishop of Canterbury, 82

Barningham, 189, 190; Adam de, 190

Barton, 102, 191

Bec, 34

Beccles, 102

Bedingfield, 101

Benedict, monk, 25; the Jew, 2. 3, 4

Beodric, 160

Beodricsworth (St. Edmund's), 160

Berdewell, 189; William de, 189

Bertrand, prior of St. Faith's, 34

Bigod, earl Roger, 91, 92, 105, 106, 188

Blakeham, Benedict de, 8

Blithing, 188

Blund, Hamo, 144; William, 189

Blunham, 188

Boxford, 96, 101

Bradfield, 96, 102, 189, 190, 191

Bretenham, 96, 101

Briddinghoe, 189

Brisewood, Hubert de, 103

Brisingeham, 188

Broc, 102; Peter de, 25

Brocford, 101

Brockdish, 190; Setphen de, 190

Brockley, 189; Reginald de, 189

Brome, 187

Bukenham, Old, 188; Radulf de, 188

Burgh, Thomas de, 193

Canterbury, 80 ff.

Cereville, Gilbert de, 111, 112

Charneles, Arnald de, 188

Chebenhall, 192

Chelsworth, 102

Chertsey, 34; abbot of, 194

Chevington, 50, 71, 101

Chipley, 189

Clare, earl de, 90, 110

Clarendon, 103

Cluny, abbot of, 194

Cokefield, 93, 102, 188, 193; Adam de, 92, 93, 153, 189, 192, 193; Robert de, 12, 15, 16, 45, 81, 92, 97, 193

Colchester, 102, 131

Coleshill, 110

Cosford, 45, 92

Cotton, 101

Coutances, Geoffrey of, 5; Walter of, bishop of Lincoln (afterwards archbishop of Rouen), 76

Coventry, 148 ff.

Dennis, cellarer, 6, 8, 9, 13, 25, 33, 34, 35, 163, 204

Dereham, 129, 132

Diceto, Ralph de, dean of London, 205

Dickleburgh, 96, 101

Diss, John de, monk, 179; William de, abbot's chaplain, 71, 177

Dover, 84

Durand, bailiff of St. Edmund's, 214

Durham, 71

Edmund, Saint, 4, 7, 16, 30, 38, 58, 82, 111, 166, 172, 174 ff.; shrine of, 3, 7, 15, 78, 86, 166 ff., 175 ff., 191

Edmund's, St. (town), 72, 73, 81, 84, 115, 119, 123, 128, 155 ff., 207 ff.

Edmund, monk, 30

Edward the Confessor, king of England, 82, 92, 103, 119

Eleanor, of Aquitaine, queen of England, 74, 75

Eleigh, 80, 81, 190; Hugh de, 190

Elmset, 113, 114

Elmswell, 71, 101, 113, 114

Elveden, Gilbert de, cellarer, 161

Ely, 132; bishops of, see Ridel, Longchamp, Eustace

Endgate, 96

Eu, 135; Roger de, 188

Eustace, 99; bishop of Ely, 207, 210, 211; monk, 26

Euston, 189

Fakenham, Great, 189
Falsham, 189
FitzAlan, Peter, 189
FitzDrogo, Richard, 72
FitzElias, cup-bearer to abbot Hugh, 70
FitzHerbert, Osbert, under sheriff, 53
FitzHervey, W., 103
FitzIsabel, William, 2
FitzPeter, Geoffrey, justiciar, 208, 211
FitzRalph, Gilbert, 97
FitzRoger, Robert, 188
FitzWalter, Robert, 189
Flaix, abbot of, 206
Flamvill, Robert de, 12
Flemetun, Allan de, 190
Fordham, Geoffrey de, 25
Fornham, the Greater, 101 ; St. Genevieve, 102 ; St. Martin, 102
Francheville, William de, 103
Fresingfield, 102

Gedding, 189
Geoffrey, archbishop of York, 32, 84, 133
Gilbert, steward of the abbey, 43 ; monk, 179
Gislingham, 101
Gissing, 188
Glanvill, Ranulf, justiciar, 11, 41, 81, 99, 115

Glemesford, 113, 210
Godfrey, bailiff of St. Edmund's, 116
Groton, 93, 102, 189, 193

Haberton, 94
Halstede, 189; Robert de, 189
Hardwick, 158
Hargrave, 50, 101
Harling, 188
Harlow, 50, 51, 98, 99, 101, 173
Hastings, Henry de, 42 ; Thomas de, 42; William de, 106, 188 ; William de, monk, 29, 30
Hatfield, Walter de, 50
Heldcercle, 102
Hengham, Hugh de, clerk, 80; Richard de, monk, 179 ; Roger de, cellarer, 6, 79, 173, 191, 192
Henry II., king of England, 24, 32ff., 75, 85, 103, 110, 119, 205
Henry of Essex, standard-bearer, afterwards a monk, 108 ff.
Hepworth, 188
Herard, 98
Herbert, the dean, 94, 95
Heribert, abbot's chaplain, afterwards prior, 195 ff.
Herlewin, 51
Hermer, novice, 25 ; subprior, 196

Herningswell, 102
Hornington, 96, 101
Hopeton, 97, 101
Horning, Robert de, 190
Horningsherth, 102, 190 ; the Greater, 101
Hostelli, Daniel de, 97
Hubert Walter, archbishop of Canterbury, 88, 105, 128 ff., 147, 180, 192
Hugh, 179 ; abbot, 1 ff., 6, 9, 10, 11, 27, 50, 60, 89, 97, 100, 114, 117, 124, 127, 128, 142, 161, 163 ; bishop of Lincoln, 148; prior, xxv., 6; third prior, 25, 26, 30, 32; sub-sacristan, afterwards sacristan, 46, 117, 125, 151, 157 ff., 171, 177, 199
Hugo, monk, 6
Hunston, 189

Icklingham, 75, 101, 209
Ickworth, 190; Richard de, 190
Ingham, 102
Ipswich, 84
Isaac, son of Rabbi Joce, 2.

Jerusalem, 63
Jocelin of Brakelond (author of the *Chronicle*), xxv., 5, 6, 20, 21 ff. ; prior's chaplain, 41 ; abbot's chaplain, 41, 55, 56, 57, 99, 100, 108 ; guest master, 151, 164 ff., 176, 201, 202

Jocell, cellarer, 179, 184, 191, 192
John, king of England, 87, 182, 211
John, bishop of Norwich, 85
John, third prior 197, 199
Jurnet, the Jew, 7

Kentford, 38
Ketel, 158
Kingston, 101
Kirkby, 188 ; Alexander de, 188

Lakford, 102
Laland, 109
Lakenheath, 161, 207 ff.
Lavenham, 189
Lea, 102
Lilesey, 189
Lincoln, 77
Livermere, 188, 190 ; Peter de, 190
Loddon, 187
London, 75, 84, 119 ff., 132, 173
Longchamp, bishop of Ely, chancellor and legate, 83, 84, 85, 129
Lovell, Ernald, 97

Malmesbury, 34
Manston, 189; Gilbert de, 189
Marlesford, 188
Marlingford, 188
Maurice, abbot's chaplain, 199

Melford, 101, 113
Mendham, 188 ; Thomas de, 91
Meringthorpe, 96, 102
Mickfield, 188
Midling, 82
Mildenhall, 73, 74, 101, 102, 125, 138, 152, 192
Monfort, Robert de, 110
Muriaux, Roger de, 190

Newton, 96, 102
Nicholas, bailiff of St. Edmund's, 114
Norfolk, 103
Nortune, 188
Norwich, 102, 105, 106, 107, 132

Oakley, 188
Octavian, anti-pope, 77
Onehouse, 189
Ording, abbot, 17, 124, 142
Oxford, 148

Pakenham, 26, 102, 191
Palegrave, 11, 66, 101
Patteshall, Simon de, 189
Peche, Gilbert de, 189
Pressenei, Ralph de, 190
Preston, 188, 190

Quiddenham, 188

Ralph, the porter, 182 ff.
Raddeston, 188

Ranulf, clerk, assistant to the cellarer, 125, 142, 143, 144, 174
Reading, 108
Rede, 188
Reydon, 188
Richard I., king of England, 74, 75 85, 134 ff., 152 ff., 181, 182, 193
Richard, archbishop of Canterbury, 5, 6, 7 ; bishop of Winchester, 32, 35, 37 ; forester 113 ; of Palegrave, 11, 66 ; monk, 177
Richingall, 101
Ridel, Geoffrey, bishop of Ely, 78, 113, 114
Risbridge, 90
Risby, 71, 102, 190 ; Norman de, 71, 190 ; William de, 71, 72
Robert, abbot, 128, 142 ; prior, xxv., 5, 12 ff., 24, 29, 32, 34, 35, 36, 138, 139, 182, 185, 194, 195 ; monk, 177
Rochester, 10
Roger, cellarer, 25, 30, 32, 139, 140, 157 ff.
Ros, Jordan de, 97, 98, 99
Rothing, 189 ; Gervase de, 189
Rougham, 102, 191
Rualdus, monk, 26
Ruffus, Geoffrey, monk, 190, 191 ; John, 204 ; Robert, monk, 12

Rungton, 51, 101
Rushbrook, 101

Saham, 101
St. Alban's, 34 ; Walter de, monk, 179
St. Andrew, chapel of, 151
St. Botolph, shrine of, 181
St. Catherine, chapel of, 151
St. Clare, Gilbert de, 189
St. Denis, chapel of, 146
St. Edmund, see Edmund
St. Faith, chapel of, 151
St. Neot's, H. de, 34
St. Nicasius, chapel of, 195
St. Robert, 23
Samson, of Tottington, abbot of St. Edmund's, (during the abbacy of abbot Hugh) 5—12, (during the vacancy in the abbey) 13—35; elected abbot, 35 ff. ; (as abbot), 40—215 ; abbot Hugh's opinion of, 9, 10 ; the monks' opinion of, 18 ; character of, by Jocelin, 62 ff. ; personal appearance of, 62 ff.
Samson, precentor, 39 ; sacristan, 48
Sapeston, 189
Saxham, 50, 101, 188, 190 ; Walter de, 190
Scaldwell, 96, 102
Scales, Robert de, 149 ; Roger de, 150

Scurun's well, 160
Semere, 93, 102, 193
Southrey, 46, 102, 161
Southwold, 192
Stanningfield, 190
Stanton, 189
Stapleford, 50, 101
Stephen, 95
Stigand, archbishop of Canterbury, 7
Stowlangtoft, 189
Stowe, 101
Stuston, 188
Stuteville, William de, 211

Tewkesbury, 193
Thelnetham, 188
Thetford, 87, 98
Thorp, 52, 101, 189, 190
Thurstan, monk, 26 ; the Little, monk, 179
Thurston, 188
Tibenham, 188
Tivetshall (Titshall), 96, 101, 107
Topescroft, 188
Tostock, William de, 188

Ulmo, Robert de, 97

Valoniis, Robert de, 97

Wachesham, Osbert de, 188
Walchelin, the archdeacon, 98
Walter, the physican, monk, 25 ; almoner, 152, 177

Waltham, 132; (Hants), 32;
  Little, 189
Wangford, 190
Warin, custodian of the shrine,
  14
Waringford, Nicholas de, 33,
  34
Warkton, 49, 102
Wattisfield, 189
Waude, 189
Wederden, 102
Weneling, 96, 102
Westley, 96, 102
Wetherden, 149
Whatefield, 189

Whelnetham, 189, 190; Geof-
  frey de, 189
Whepstead, 8, 102
William, sacristan, 2 ff,. 13, 15,
  16, 25, 33, 34, 46, 47, 48;
  bishop of Norwich, 97
Wimer, sheriff, 39
Windsor, 87
Witham, 90
Woolpit, 76 ff., 101
Wordwell, 190; William de,
  190
Worlingworth, 101
Wortham, 101, 188,
Wrabnesse, 102